THE AUTHOR

R. B. McDowell is a Fellow of Trinity College, University of Dublin. He is the author of several historical studies, including *The Irish Administration* (Routledge, 1964), *Alice Stopford Green, a Passionate Historian* (Alan Figgis, 1967), and, with R. B. Stanford, *Mahaffy: A Biography of an Anglo-Irishman* (Routledge, 1971). Reviewing *The Irish Convention 1917-18* (1970), Professor McDowell's previous book in the 'Studies in Irish History' series, the *Economic and Social Review* commented: 'This continuously interesting book has been splendidly researched. The extensive bibliography shows how widely and deeply Professor McDowell has cast his

VOLUME X

THE CHURCH OF IRELAND
1869–1969

STUDIES IN IRISH HISTORY, SECOND SERIES

THE CHURCH
OF IRELAND
1869–1969

by

R. B. McDOWELL

Routledge & Kegan Paul

LONDON AND BOSTON

1975

First published in 1975
by Routledge & Kegan Paul Ltd
Broadway House, 68–74 Carter Lane,
London EC4V 5EL and
9 Park Street,
Boston, Mass. 02108, USA
Set in Monotype Baskerville
and printed in Great Britain by
Cox & Wyman Ltd,
London, Fakenham and Reading

ISBN 0 7100 8072 7

CONTENTS

ACKNOWLEDGMENTS

SOME YEARS AGO I was requested by the Archbishop of Armagh, the Most Reverend G. O. Simms, to write this account of the Church of Ireland during the century following disestablishment. The staff of the representative church body and of its library have been most helpful, but I alone am responsible for the views expressed.

I am most grateful to my colleague Professor T. W. Moody, to Professor J. C. Beckett, to the Right Reverend Robert Wyse Jackson and to Dr K. Milne for reading the work and for valuable criticism. I wish to thank Mr B. M. Walker, Miss C. Gardiner and Miss N. O'Sullivan for their assistance. I also wish to thank the Public Record Office of Northern Ireland and the trustees of the British Museum for permission to use material in their collections.

INTRODUCTION

~~~~~~

THE CHURCH OF IRELAND is a small church in a small country
and, during the past hundred years having been neither rent
asunder by schisms nor distressed by heresies, it has had a
peaceful, uneventful history. But just over a century ago when
it sustained the double shock of disestablishment and partial
disendowment, its adherents were suddenly forced to accept the
freedom, responsibilities and burdens associated with membership of a voluntary church. Then, in the years following disestablishment, the Church of Ireland had to adapt itself to
striking changes in the geographical distribution of its membership, and in the pattern of Irish society. At the time of disestablishment it was still the church of the Irish ruling world,
including in its membership nearly all the greater Irish
landowners, the bulk of the landed gentry, and a high proportion
of the professional and business classes. But the Irish landlords
have been bought out, and, taking Ireland as a whole, the
relative importance of episcopalians in business and professional
life has declined. Not only has the Church of Ireland had to
face and cope with change. For centuries its members have
formed a distinctive and influential element in a complex
community. Even in areas where the Church of Ireland is weak,
the rector has been an important local figure, and his small
congregation, with theological and political loyalties sharply
different from those prevailing round them, have brought a
stimulating variety to local life. What is most significant, and
yet hardest to assess and describe, is the impact the church has
made on the spiritual life of its members. All that can be said

ix

here is that in a study inevitably concerned with details of organization, general policy and the pressures of secular politics, one factor looms impressively large – the earnest and self-sacrificing devotion to their church displayed by many members of the Church of Ireland.

I

THE CHURCH OF IRELAND IN THE MID-NINETEENTH CENTURY

~~~~~~~~~~~~~~~~~~~~~~~~~~~~~~~~~~~~~~~

ABOUT THE MIDDLE of the nineteenth century the members of the Church of Ireland were both convinced that their church could claim to be the ancient church of Ireland, founded by St Patrick in the fifth century, and were thankful that it formed part of the anglican communion, to the tradition of which the church of Ussher and Berkeley had not failed to make its contribution. They were also very conscious that their church was an established church, privileged and bearing a grave responsibility for the spiritual welfare of the community. To be precise, the Church of Ireland was a branch of an established church, the united church of England and Ireland which came into being in January 1801. This union indeed had little practical significance, however reassuring it might be to the members of the smaller church. Englishmen were occasionally – less often than in the past – appointed to Irish sees, and Irish clergymen began to go in increasing numbers to English parishes. But the union of the churches of England and Ireland was not expressed through any institutional links. Each church had its own court of final appeal in ecclesiastical causes, this being in Ireland delegates in chancery,[1] and in England delegates in chancery until 1832 and thereafter the privy council. When the union was under consideration, it was suggested that the two branches of the united church should have a common legislative and deliberative assembly, it being provided in the articles of union as first drafted that, when the crown summoned a convocation, the bishops and clergy of the Irish provinces should sit in 'the convocation of the united church'. But when the articles were being debated at Westminster, it was realized that there were in fact two convocations in England, and the reference to the representation of the Irish church in convocation was deleted.

In the late twelfth century the synod of Cashel, held shortly after Henry's II's arrival in Ireland, declared that 'the divine offices should be celebrated in every part of Ireland according to the forms and usages of the Church of England', and from early in the sixteenth century the Irish church, in doctrine and discipline, conformed closely to the pattern set by the Church of England. The ecclesiastical legislation of the last four Tudor sovereigns was duplicated in Ireland; during the early Stuart period Calvinist and Arminian strove within the Irish church; Ireland had its restoration settlement, its Caroline act of uniformity and later its non-jurors, silenced convocation, toleration act and ecclesiastical Augustan age. But there was one great and striking difference between the established churches of England and Ireland. From the reformation, the Church of England embraced the majority of Englishmen (however varied the intensities of their theological loyalties). The Church of Ireland on the other hand was the church of a small minority of the population, a minority which, even a cursory observer could see, was distributed very unevenly both geographically and socially. To explain this would involve a long excursus into two or three centuries of Irish history. At this point it must suffice to say that in 1871 the members of the established church amounted to 667,900 out of a population of 5,412,000. That is to say they were just under one-eighth of the total population (12·34 per cent). And it may be added that such statistics as we have suggest that the members of the established church had never amounted to more than about one-eighth of the population of Ireland. Certainly by 1871 its position seemed almost static, because the previous census, that of 1861, which had supplied the first reliable Irish religious statistics, showed that the members of the established church, 693,300 in number, amounted to 11·96 per cent of the population.

The geographical distribution of the Church of Ireland population was remarkably unequal. It comprised in Ulster 21·5 per cent of the population, in Leinster 12·3 per cent, in Munster 5·3 per cent and in Connaught 4·2 per cent. Generally speaking, the church's membership tended to be concentrated in the north and east, thinning out towards the south and west. Its distribution in fact reflected the success of settlement and plantation and the power of the crown in the reformation and counter-reformation age; thus half the membership of the established church was to be found in Ulster, the most thoroughly planted province, and it was comparatively strong in the old Pale area and the prosperous parts of the great central plain, where the colony had maintained itself in the later middle ages. One Ulster county, Down, had the largest number of episcopalians (60,000) and another, Fermanagh, the highest proportion of episcopalians (37 per cent) among the Irish counties. In no Ulster county did the episcopalians sink below 12 per cent, and in none of the other counties, with the exception of Dublin (19 per cent), and Wicklow (17 per cent) did they rise above 12 per cent of the population. The distribution of the membership of the established church was influenced by two other factors. Irish protestantism, relatively strong in the business and professional worlds, had an urban bias, and here and there a large estate may for a time have been a force favouring protestantism.

But the simple figure of one-eighth of the population did not apply with anything approaching consistency to the occupational groups listed in the census. To begin with, of the landowners recorded in the census, 50 per cent were members of the established church. And this figure in fact seriously underrates the strength of the established church in the landed world. As the census commissioners themselves stated, their returns were misleading on this subject. There was, they wrote, 'some considerable vice of excess through misapprehension of the strict meaning of landed proprietor'. It was clear, the commissioners went on to say, 'that the acreage of land in protestant episcopalian ownership exceeds so largely the surface under all other proprietorship as to constitute the landed

3

proprietory of the country episcopalian protestant by emphasis'.
It is scarcely necessary to say more, but two other indications of
the close alliance between episcopalianism and landowning
may be mentioned. In the early 1880s over 70 per cent of the
justices of the peace in the counties were members of the
Church of Ireland. And about the same time 250 members of
the general synod between them owned over 1,000,000 acres.[2]

In the 1870s the landlords were still a potent force in Irish
life, economically powerful and politically and socially self-
confident. The landed classes ranged from peers possessing tens
of thousands of acres, through respectable, established county
families to gentlemen farmers and squireens with a few hundred
acres, but all living in a very different social and economic
climate from that of the tenant farmers, often with very small
holdings, by which they were surrounded. As Archdeacon
Grantly pointed out about 1867:[3]

It is a comfortable feeling to know you stand on your own ground.
Land is about the only thing that can't fly away. And then you see
land gives so much more than the rent. It gives position and political
power, to say nothing about the game.

In fact an Irish landlord in his 'big house' not only controlled
an economic unit, his estate, but was expected to advise and
help his tenants and take an active part in local affairs. 'A
country gentleman', a country clergyman wrote:[4]

as a member of a grand jury . . . levied the local taxes, appointed
the nephews of his old friends to collect them, and spent them when
they were gathered in. He controlled the boards of guardians, and
appointed the dispensary doctors, regulated the diet of paupers,
inflicted fines and administered the law at petty sessions.

In addition, until the ballot act of 1872 and the representation
of the people act of 1884 greatly changed the conditions under
which Irish elections were fought, the Irish county seats were
usually won by men belonging to landed families. The landed
world had immense influence. A landlord's way of life, with its
privileges and responsibilities, affording, as it did, independence,
leisure and opportunities for manly sports, provided the most
favourable environment for the production of a gentleman. And
gentlemen, the Victorians firmly believed, should be the
natural leaders and guardians of the community. In Ireland the

landlords controlled county government, managed local charities, officered the militia and ran the hunts and race meetings, and their younger sons and many small landowners entered the professions and helped to set the standards of conduct over wide areas of Irish life.

Episcopalian predominance in the landed world influenced the denominational balance in many sections of the Irish social structure. It is scarcely surprising that of the gentlemen and gentlewomen of independent means (a category in which women outnumbered men by three to one) 55 per cent were members of the Church of Ireland. On the other hand, in the next category in the census tables, 'vagrants' (in which again women predominated in a ratio of three to one), episcopalians were only 4 per cent. It is also significant that while only 7 per cent of the 335,000 female domestic servants were episcopalian, 19 per cent of the 27,000 male domestic servants were Church of Ireland. The professions were to a great extent recruited from the landed world and largely dependent on it, so naturally enough the Church of Ireland was strongly represented in the professional sections of Irish society. Its membership included one-third of the clergy of all denominations; 80 per cent of the serving and 60 per cent of the retired army officers; 60 per cent of the barristers and over 50 per cent of the solicitors (nearly 60 per cent of the two branches of the profession combined); 50 per cent of the civil engineers; and just under 50 per cent of the medical men and architects. Of teachers in Ireland — school-masters, schoolmistresses and governesses – about 30 per cent were members of the Church of Ireland. Of the more bohemian, or at least less formally organized professions, the Church of Ireland had more than its proportionate share, with 28 per cent of the actors and actresses, 38 per cent of the painters, sculptors and engravers, and 38 per cent of the comparatively new craft of photographers. The Church of Ireland's long-standing connection with the state was represented by the fact that still in 1871 about 38 per cent of those who returned them-selves as civil servants were members of the Church of Ireland. And 25 per cent of the police and over 60 per cent of the rank and file of the army stationed in Ireland were episcopalians.

The Church of Ireland was also disproportionately strong in some spheres of Irish business life. Fifty-four per cent of those concerned with banking, 30 per cent of the accountants and of the commercial travellers, 26 per cent of the merchants, 23 per cent of the commercial clerks, 21 per cent of the brokers and auctioneers were members of the Church of Ireland. In retail trade the Church of Ireland seems to have been relatively weak. Only 8 per cent of those who returned themselves as 'shop-keeper' were episcopalian. And in the other large occupation groups engaged in retail trade, the Church of Ireland tended to be under-represented. Episcopalians amounted to only 6·5 per cent of butchers and poulterers, 5 per cent of fishmongers, a little over 4 per cent of hucksters, and less than 4 per cent of green-grocers, though they had their correct proportion of grocers (12·9 per cent), and of pawnbrokers (13 per cent), and were over-represented amongst booksellers (25 per cent), wine and spirit merchants (19 per cent) and gunsmiths (31 per cent).

Episcopalians were strong in one section of Irish industry, the textile manufactures, comprising about 20 per cent of the workers employed – about 90 per cent of the Church of Ireland textile workers being in Ulster. The main Irish industry was, of course, agriculture and there were in Ireland in 1871 42,000 farmers and graziers who were members of the Church of Ireland. It was a substantial number, but it must be quickly pointed out that it represented just under 10 per cent of the total numbers of farmers and graziers in Ireland. There were also 54,000 Church of Ireland farm labourers, again a substantial number, but only 6·4 per cent of the total number in Ireland. As might be expected, the bulk of the episcopalian farmers and farm workers were in the north, there being in the province of Ulster 29,000 farmers and 32,000 agricultural labourers who were members of the Church of Ireland.

The ecclesiastical organization of the Church of Ireland reflected its medieval origins. Diocesan and parochial boun-daries had been shaped by historic forces working over centuries. Endowments, the fruits of past enterprise and beneficence, had often ceased to bear a realistic relationship to contemporary needs. The income of the parochial clergy, largely derived from tithe and glebe lands, was distributed erratically in relation to the work to be done. And although, owing to appropriations in the past, the tithe of a parish did not always go to its own incumbent, the income of a living, whatever might be its source, was a vested interest protected by law, principle and prejudice. The nineteenth century, however, was an age in which there was a growing belief in the virtues of economy, fairness and efficiency, when keen reformers, angered by abuses and anomalies – however picturesque – were eager to make the best use of all available resources. The Church of Ireland was affected by these forces. At the beginning of the nineteenth century it comprised, strictly speaking, thirty-five dioceses, though it had only twenty-two diocesans – four archbishops and eighteen bishops – in a number of instances more than one diocese being governed by a single bishop. But one of the first measures of the first reformed parliament, the Irish ecclesiastical temporalities act of 1833 which began the process of rationalizing the Church of Ireland's organization, abolished two archbishoprics and provided that ten dioceses should each be united on the next vacancy to a neighbouring see. As a result, by 1850, when the act became fully effective with the death of the bishop of Clogher, the Church of Ireland episcopate was reduced to twelve – the archbishops of Armagh and Dublin and ten bishops. The diocesan pattern was varied by the fact that, while those dioceses which had been united to a neighbouring diocese in the pre-reformation era were for practical purposes geographical expressions (their former status reflected only in a small cathedral, or the titles of some dignitaries), the dioceses which were united after 1833 retained their consistory courts.

The members of the Irish bench sat in the house of lords in rotation (an archbishop and three bishops attending for a session at a time) and they naturally lived in some state. Though the ecclesiastical temporalities act had shorn them of much of their wealth, their incomes in the sixties were still substantial. The archbishop of Armagh had a net income of nearly £10,000 per annum, the archbishop of Dublin had over £7,000, the bishop of Derry had over £6,000 and the remaining nine bishops enjoyed on an average £3,850 per annum. In comparison the lord chancellor's income was £8,000, a common law puisne judge was paid about £3,700 per annum and the under-secretary, the permanent head of the Irish administration, had a salary of £2,000. In a landed society it was accepted by many that a bishop should have the status of a large landowner. 'I for one', a very outspoken member of the bench remarked,[5] am not disposed to undervalue the rank and dignity which the state, more for her own honour than for ours, has bestowed upon the episcopate. As a matter of individual taste I infinitely prefer a carriage bishop to a gig bishop.

The Irish bench in 1868 was an impressive body, comprising a number of men of definite character, some of whom were distinguished by their literary or oratorical powers. The primate, Marcus Gervais Beresford, belonged to a family 'connected for generations with the highest dignity and power in the civil and ecclesiastical administration of Ireland',[6] and he was closely related to three distinguished Irishmen, John Beresford, Grattan and Bushe. His instinctive self-assurance and dignity of bearing, allied as they were to firmness, tact and kindliness, made him a respected leader of his church in difficult times. Two of his suffragans, Knox and Bernard, also belonged by birth to the Irish ruling world. Knox, bishop of Down, the grandson of the first Viscount Northland, the son of an archdeacon and the nephew of a bishop, was a quiet, restrained man (Matthew Arnold spoke of him as being the least assertive prelate he knew).[7] But during his tenure of the united diocese new parishes were formed and a number of churches built, and Knox, with calm tenacity, maintained his whig principles in an unsympathetic environment. Bernard of Tuam was a brother of the earl of Bandon. Described by an admirer as being 'the perfect example of a true Irish gentleman', pre-eminent for his 'solidity', he was responsible for greatly enlarging Tuam cathedral and seems to have been a very competent diocesan administrator.[8]

Six of the bench were scholars or men of letters. Of these the best known was Trench, who had been appointed archbishop of Dublin in 1863. At Cambridge a member of the brilliant and high-spirited circle which included John Sterling and Arthur Hallam, Trench was a man of poetic sensitivity and generous enthusiasms. As a young man he had gone to Spain to fight for the liberal cause. Theologically he was a high churchman, the correspondent of Samuel Wilberforce, but he was also a friend of Maurice, the great broad-churchman. He was a prolific writer, easy to read, with a wide range of interests – poetry, theology, history, literature – who wrote for a wide public: he was capable of producing lectures on philology which were both instructive and entertaining. In 1856 he became dean of Westminster, and on Whately's death he was appointed arch-bishop of Dublin. English opinion highly approved of the appointment – Trench was broad-minded, conciliatory, aware of contemporary trends and a member of a well-known Irish family. But the *Saturday Review* wondered whether 'a poetical and somewhat dreamy mind' was fitted for coping with 'the lowering looks of an embittered clergy, a fanatical laity and the outposts of a hostile camp'.[9] Trench himself accepted the archbishopric 'not with pleasure but as a matter of duty'. 'England', he wrote,[10]

is my world, the land of all my friends, the English church seems to me to feel full of life and hope and vigour, of which I see little in Ireland. Then . . . I see myself deficient in some of the most needful qualities for the episcopate. I have few or no gifts of government, little or no power of rallying men round me, and disciplining them into harmonious action.

In fact, as archbishop of Dublin, Trench displayed adminis-trative ability, courage and wide sympathies, and he made an inestimable contribution to the Church of Ireland in a formative era. But, a man of peace with a pessimistic strain, he suffered acutely during the fervent and occasionally acrimonious debates on disestablishment and prayer-book revision. And after disestablishment he was very conscious (as he perhaps somewhat tactlessly declared) that 'Ireland is provincial and is growing more provincial every day'.[11]

Alexander of Derry resembled Trench in more than one respect. Though his family was Irish he had been educated in England, and he too was a poet and a high churchman. But he had a buoyant temperament and a quick sense of humour and he was very ready to fight with gusto for his convictions. Genial and charming, Alexander possessed a poetic sensitivity, a mas-culine understanding and a mastery of language which made him one of the most eloquent speakers and preachers of his day.

Four of the bishops had been university dons. Fitzgerald of Killaloe had been professor of moral philosophy in Trinity, and Butcher of Meath, Graves of Limerick and O'Brien of Ossory were sometime fellows. Fitzgerald was undoubtedly able and had an impressive list of publications to his credit in spite of 'a besetting indolence' which annoyed his friends.[12] Butcher had been a level-headed regius professor of divinity; as a bishop, it was said, he never left his books, entrusting diocesan administration largely to his energetic archdeacon, Stopford.[13] Graves was the admirable Crichton of the bench. A mathematician of ability and a pioneer in Irish archaeology, as a young man, being intended for the army 'he became an expert swordsman and rider; he played cricket for his university and later in life did much boating and fly-fishing'. Also he was the only prelate who, on making a return of his income to the established church commission of 1867, mentioned that he paid a secretary, an expenditure he considered unavoidable, 'in order to transact properly the diocesan business'. O'Brien, an able theologian – his work on justification ran into several editions – had the curious fate for a bishop of being the subject of an uncomplimentary biography, the work of Carroll, an eccentric Dublin clergyman who apparently admired O'Brien. According to Carroll, O'Brien's great faults as a bishop were his 'dilatoriness and inhospitality'. His 'pride and hauteur', Carroll generously granted, arose from his inability to overcome his shyness and social timidity, and he was, Carroll had to admit, 'free from the sin of nepotism except perhaps in two or three instances in which connections of his wife obtained unusually rapid promotion'.[14] Carroll's bitterness evinces the strength of O'Brien's personality, and even this over-candid biographer had to admit that O'Brien was a man of tremendous industry with a strong independent mind. Moreover, he was always ready to speak out clearly and courageously on controversial issues.

O'Brien was one of the four outstanding evangelicals on the Irish bench, the others being Verschoyle of Kilmore, Daly of Cashel and Gregg of Cork. Verschoyle had been for years, at the episcopal chapel in Baggot Street, one of the leading evangelical preachers in Dublin. Daly was a forcible preacher, full of urgent concern for his hearers; so plain-spoken and direct that his devoted biographer was constrained to admit that he sometimes seemed ill-tempered. But he was undoubtedly a warmhearted man, eager, as he showed at the time of the Famine, to help his fellows.[15] Gregg, a younger man by fifteen years, was a friend of Daly's. He too was a vigorous preacher (if need be in Irish). Cheerfulness marked his preaching. 'Look forward', he declared, 'to a coming eternity with a high hearted hope.' And

his advice on preaching to a country congregation is characteristic. 'Short sermon', he wrote, 'thirty-five minutes, explain
text, reason on it, urge it home strongly, exhort warmly,
conclude prayfully and close simply.'[16]

The parochial clergy of the Church of Ireland in the 1860s
numbered just over 2,000 – 1,500 incumbents and about 500
curates. Both the distribution of the clergy and their incomes
bore little relation to the work they had to do.[17] As has been said,
parochial boundaries had been shaped by historic forces. They
also, to some extent, revealed the distribution of economic
resources or agricultural productivity at the time they were
settled, and they reflected the fact that the church believed that it
must, if possible, place its ministrations within reasonable reach
of every member of the whole community. The beneficed
parochial clergy were distributed on a geographical basis,
there being in the province of Armagh 621; in Dublin 325; in
Cashel 441; and in Tuam 131. As a result an incumbent in the
diocese of Down, Connor and Dromore had on an average
1,000 Church of Ireland parishioners, an incumbent in the
diocese of Tuam had on average 180, and an incumbent in the
united diocese of Cashel, Emly, Waterford and Lismore had
fewer than 135. There were indeed 201 benefices, the great
majority in the three southern provinces, with a Church of
Ireland population of under 40. The employment of curates did
little to equalize the work. If in Down and Connor and Dromore
there were 48 curates, Ossory, Ferns and Leighlin, with about a
quarter of the episcopalian population of the northern united
diocese, had 59. In Cashel, Emly and Lismore there were 31
curates and even Tuam had 9. After all it was for the incumbent
who paid the curate's salary to decide whether or not a curate
should be employed in his parish.

Clerical incomes varied erratically and had little relation to
the number of Church of Ireland parishioners. An estimate
made in 1868 of the net incomes of incumbents (including the
value of the glebe house but deducting a salary paid to a curate,
gave 109 incumbents as having incomes of over £500 per
annum (seven had incomes of over £1,000); 688 had incomes of
between £200 and £500 a year (333 having over £300) and
720 – just under 40 per cent – had incomes of under £200
(including 300 incumbents whose incomes were under £100

per annum). As for curates, their salaries were usually not less than £75, nor more than £100 per annum, and it seems that they did not always receive their stipends with unfailing punctuality. On the other hand, rectors could be exacting. Edward Maguire records that when he went to his first curacy, which was in Donegal, his rector, having received him 'very graciously' told him that if he left the parish for a single day without leave he would prosecute him. He then intimated to Maguire that he was to preach on the following Sunday. Having heard the sermon the rector informed Maguire that he himself was leaving for a short holiday – which lasted for ten months.[18] It is not therefore altogether surprising that in 1868 Butcher, bishop of Meath, who when regius professor of divinity had been in close touch with divinity students, should have drawn attention to the need to increase curates' stipends. And he suggested that a single curate might be employed by two or more incumbents.[19] However, Irish curates were fortunate in two respects. The proportion of curates to incumbents was fairly low, and about two-thirds of the Irish benefices were in the gift of an archbishop or bishop. Curates (and the poorer incumbents) could therefore hope for promotion if their merits were appreciated when episcopal patronage was being distributed.

When considering clerical incomes it is interesting to see how they compared with the incomes of some other occupations. The headmasters of the larger Irish grammar schools were paid between £400 and £500 per annum, their assistants were paid between £150 and £200; resident magistrates were paid between £378 and £578; local government board inspectors were paid between £350 and £650 and of the 42 agents of the Bank of Ireland, 21 were paid between £300 and £400, and only two were paid more than £500 per annum. Finally, it may be added that the number of persons in Ireland assessed to income tax under schedules D and E with income of over £200 amounted to about 8,600.

A high proportion of the clergy had the status conferred by the possession of a cathedral stall. The Church of Ireland had no fewer than thirty-three cathedrals. Thirty-one dioceses had a cathedral each, and Dublin had two, St Patrick's and Christ Church. Of these cathedrals five were in ruins and few of the others were of cathedral proportions by English or European standards. Thirteen indeed were parish churches and in only a few were daily choral services maintained. But no fewer than thirty of the cathedrals had deans and chapters. There was one cathedral without a dean (Aghadoe), and two deans (Kilmore and Ardagh) with a cathedral but without a chapter and finally the diocese of Meath, though it lacked a cathedral, had a dean (Clonmacnoise) as well as an archdeacon. There was also the dean of the chapel royal, in Dublin Castle, an office which was to continue as a vestigial remnant of the establishment until 1922.[20] So there were in all thirty-three deans, thirty-three archdeacons, about seventy other dignitaries, and over 170 canons and prebendaries. The archdeacons, of course, played a useful part in diocesan administration and the deans managed their cathedrals (the services in practice being often taken by a local clergyman), but the remaining dignitaries had few or no duties attached to their stalls. It may be added that, while a few of the deans had substantial *ex officio* incomes, the other cathedral clergy received little or nothing in virtue of their stalls. As the bishops stated in 1864, the existence of numerous cathedrals 'gave the church establishment a semblance of wealth and grandeur unsuited to and at variance with its actual conditions'[21] – though it must have been a source of gratification to many individuals.

Taken as a body, the clergy of the establishment were certainly not wealthy. Some of them indeed were poor. But most of them had, or could look forward to having, a reasonable middle-class income. Moreover, they enjoyed considerable social prestige. They were with very few exceptions university men (the non-graduates seem to have amounted to a little over 1 per cent of the total) and they were often connected by family ties and their way of life with the landed gentry. It has been easy to discover the occupations or status of the fathers of about 1,300 of the 1,500 clergymen who were incumbents in 1868 – though it must be admitted that a father's occupation (especially when expressed in its Latin form) is sometimes an uncertain indication of his status or economic standing. Of those whose fathers' professions are known, fifteen were the sons of peers or baronets (in fact a viscount and a courtesy earl were deans in the west of Ireland, Lord Mountmorres being dean of Achonry and Lord Chichester, the heir to the marquis of Donegall, being dean of Raphoe). Just over 27 per cent belonged to families which clearly regarded themselves as established, the father being described in the Trinity College entrance book as 'armiger', 'generosus' (gentleman), private gentleman or high sheriff. The term 'gentleman' was, of course, loosely defined and subjectively applied. But in a status-conscious society there was probably considerable reluctance to incur the contempt which would be aroused by presumptuous assertiveness, and many of those who used the term in the Trinity College entrance book were indubitably members of landed families. Over half (55 per cent) of the incumbents were the sons of professional men, army and naval officers, lawyers (including judges), medical men (including the president of the Royal College of Surgeons), civil servants (revenue officials, clerks in government office and an official of the East India company), schoolmasters, two provosts of Trinity, Dublin, and clergymen. Just half of the incumbents whose fathers were professional men were the sons of clergymen (including a methodist, a presbyterian and a moravian minister), and about twenty were the sons of bishops. Only a small number (almost 11 per cent) were the sons of business men – bankers, merchants, manufacturers, and an occasional shopkeeper. A much smaller number (just over 4 per cent) were farmers' sons. Of the clergy who had attended a university, 90 per cent had been to Trinity College, Dublin. The remainder included a sprinkling of Oxford and Cambridge men, a rare graduate of another British university, for instance London or Glasgow, and even a vicar, Reichel of Mullingar, who had begun his university career at Berlin. Possibly because of this unusual academic background, Reichel had the temerity to point out to archbishop Whately a serious weakness in one of the archbishop's favourite aphorisms on biblical criticism. Whately acknowledged the force of Reichel's argument but thenceforth 'never treated the young clergyman with the old cordiality'.

Trinity College, with its divinity school, was a most important factor in the life of the Church of Ireland. About 80 per cent of its undergraduates were members of the established church. Chapel and catechetical lectures – both compulsory for members of the Church of Ireland – the predominance of clerical fellows, the portraits in the examination theatre, all reminded students that Trinity was a place of religious as well as secular learning. A substantial proportion of graduates (in the years before disestablishment about one-third) took orders, and Trinity provided the great majority of the Church of Ireland clergy with a common intellectual background and a common academic environment, which, with its work, sport and talk, they shared with those who, as laymen, were to play an active part in the life of their church.

The divinity school impressed on its pupils the churchmanship associated with the Irish establishment. It goes without saying that it was strongly protestant, and that its protestantism was definitely tinctured with evangelicalism, since the Church of Ireland had been profoundly influenced by the evangelical revival. About the middle of the century, evangelicals were prominent in many church societies; most of the leading preachers in the metropolis were noted evangelicals; in 1842 a prominent evangelical was for the first time placed on the bench, and many of the clergy, who would not have designated themselves evangelicals in the party sense, were in some degree affected by the movement. But the outlook of the divinity school was also influenced by its academic background and by the traditions of the establishment. It attached great importance to sound learning; and it had a respect for order and decorum, a distaste for extremes and an instinctive wish to extend the boundaries of comprehension as far as firmly held convictions would permit.

The divinity school provided a two-year course, with lectures and examinations, leading to the divinity testimonium, which a very large number of candidates for orders in the Church of Ireland obtained. The university also conferred the degrees of BD and DD. These degrees, it was pointed out in 1852, were granted without 'the application of any real test'. All that was required was 'the lapse of a certain time', payment of certain fees and the performance of formal exercises. In the middle 1870s, however – presumably at Salmon's suggestion – an examination was instituted for the degree of BD and candidates for the degree of DD were required to submit a thesis. In the early 1850s it was proposed that efforts should be made 'to invest' the divinity school 'with a practical character'. It was suggested that a chair of pastoral theology should be founded

and arrangements made for divinity students to work in a
selected parish under supervision, it being pointed out that some
of them were already working as Sunday school teachers or
under the parochial visitors' society. Lord John George
Beresford, the primate, was very critical of these suggestions.
He drew attention to the danger that divinity students might be
diverted from their academic work and he was afraid that the
parish selected as a training ground would soon be 'in a forced
and artificial state of spiritual cultivation'.[22] In fact thirty-five
years were to elapse before a professorship of pastoral theology
was added to the school. When it was founded in 1888 it was
provided that the holder should be elected for five years by the
bishops of the Church of Ireland, and the chair has been held
by a succession of well-known parish clergymen, of whom five
have become diocesan bishops.

The staff of the divinity school consisted of the regius professor of divinity and archbishop King's lecturer (this lecture-
ship being raised to a professorship in 1906) and their assistants –
these until the close of the 1870s being always fellows – together
with the recently founded professorships of biblical Greek and
ecclesiastical history. In addition there were three other professorships closely associated with the divinity school – the
professorships of moral philosophy, Hebrew and Irish, the
successive holders of the chair of Irish being for nearly a century
after its foundation Church of Ireland clergymen. In the early
1860s the regius professor was Butcher, a learned and level-
headed teacher. His colleague as archbishop King's lecturer was
William Lee, from 1864 archdeacon of Dublin, an erudite and
fiery high churchman, an indefatigable parish clergyman and
defender of his faith, one of the company of revisers, and on visits
to London a strenuous conversationalist in the Athenaeum.[23]
When, in 1866, Butcher was appointed bishop of Meath, he was
succeeded as regius professor by George Salmon, a towering
personality in church and college. Salmon, at the time of his
appointment, had attained considerable distinction as a
mathematician, and he had published a number of sermons in
which he had shown himself capable of grappling with major
theological problems. Gifted with a masculine intellect, he was
generous and gentle, but his kindliness was strongly impregnated with dashes of sardonic humour. As a theologian he

belonged to the common-sense school, and a devoted pupil who praised him for never shirking difficulties implies that Salmon's forte lay in critical analysis rather than in constructive synthesis. But Salmon's critical acumen was exercised against the background of a firmly grounded Christian faith which enabled him to face the intellectual problems of his day with steadfast confidence. Fundamentally he was a strong protestant, averse to sentimentality, quick to scrutinize the claims of ecclesiastical authority and contemptuous of ritualism. He was, however, both learned and cultured; his interests were wide and his sympathies broadened rather than narrowed with age. He even hoped that his *The infallibility of the church*, a powerful addition to polemical theology, would assist in removing 'what is now the greatest obstacle to the union of Christians'. And five years after he published it he wrote to a close friend, 'I have been in several fights and have sometimes given hard knocks, but I have always been glad to make peace because I have found the giving usually pains myself as much as the adversary'.[24] Salmon was a commanding teacher, lucid in exposition with shrewd touches which illuminated his argument and helped to hold the attention of his listeners. Such a man was certain to have immense influence on his students, and through them on the church at large. And he undoubtedly strengthened the Trinity divinity school tradition of respect for sound scholarship combined with a cautious comprehensiveness in approaching theological development and change.

Once ordained, many of the Church of Ireland clergy had to face an acute problem – under-employment. In two-thirds of the total number of parishes the members of the Church of Ireland amounted to fewer than 500 persons, in nearly one-third of the parishes they were fewer than 100, though admittedly it was sometimes pointed out that the extent of the area to be covered, as well as the number of parishioners, should be taken into account in estimating the amount of work to be done. Even so, a paucity of Church of Ireland parishioners could be most discouraging. Achilles Daunt, the great evangelical preacher, as a young man showed himself at Rincurran to be an active parish clergyman, organizing village prayer meetings and confirmation classes for servants. After a few years there he was appointed to Ballymoney in the south-west of county Cork with a net income of £460. On his arrival he was greeted with the information 'that there was a fine new house and forty acres of prime land' attached to the living, in short 'every comfort that a gentleman could desire'. But he found that the Church of Ireland parishioners numbered only 260, and having 'an almost morbid sensitiveness of conscience', Daunt found that 'the very richness of the emolument' added 'poignancy to the pain'.[25] Paucity of numbers, it was pointed out, also created a problem for the preacher. He could preach against sin in a general way, but could not preach against any particular sin without apparently attacking one or two individuals in the congregation.[26] Fitzgerald, when bishop of Cork, referred to the problem of clerical under-employment in his first charge, 'I owe', he wrote,[27]

it is natural that a man of shining talents and great energies should feel disheartened when he finds his lot cast in a remote place and among a few ignorant people, and it is natural also that an indolent man should encourage himself to do nothing.

A shrewd observer of contemporary clerical life put it more bluntly. The Irish clergyman, Anthony Trollope wrote, was 'a sincere man with strong convictions'. He was 'always active, though unfortunately his activity has but a small field of usefulness'. There was nothing more depressing for a man, Trollope added, 'than a doubt whether or no he truly earns the bread which he eats'.[28]

It was, of course, strongly asserted that even in a parish with a proportionately very small Church of Ireland population, a resident incumbent had a most useful part to play in the social life of the whole community. An active-minded clergyman, Warburton, the dean of Elphin, who had about a hundred protestant parishioners, explained to Gladstone that 'my Roman catholic neighbours are in the habit of coming to me for advice, for "characters" and for assistance in temporal matters, and I have never refused to render them every reasonable assistance in my power'. Warburton explained that he managed a national school and he believed that 'the poor Roman catholics of this neighbourhood would be very sorry to have me *abolished* . . . where there are no resident gentry I believe the presence of a parochial minister to be a very great advan-

tage'.[29] The *Saturday Review*, with its refusal to sentimental-
ize, expressed the same view rather differently: 'Although the Irish
protestant clergyman has no opportunity of offering his spiritual ministrations, yet he cheers the local society by wearing a
tolerably good coat and is a free purchaser of butter and eggs.'[30]

But when they had the opportunity, many of the clergy were
extremely hard-working. As early as the 1830s Belfast, with its
steadily growing Church of Ireland population, offered a field
to a vigorous worker, and Thomas Drew, the first incumbent
of the new parish of Christ Church, which included a maze of
working-class streets on the west of the town, seized his opportunity. As soon as his church was completed in 1833 he started
schools and Sunday schools, issued the Christ Church psalm
and hymn book, and founded a library and a juvenile library –
adults paying five shillings and juveniles a penny a year. From
time to time the parish organized great parades and picnics
for the children. On Easter Monday 1844, for instance, a long
procession marched to the country, and 'the free and bounding
air of the hills as it breathed upon these children of the loom
and factory was welcomed with delight'. Drew's activities were
not limited to his own parish. He played a leading part in the
foundation of the Magdalene asylum and the formation of the
Down and Connor clergy aid society 'for the purpose of
endeavouring to supply by co-operative exertion the deficiencies
of ministerial attention'. Believing that 'the drama is the most
dangerous portion of our literature' together with 'all the
accomplishments – the hours, the assembly . . . the songs, the
dancing, the levity of conduct and dress of the figurants', he
urged the Belfast newspapers not to publish theatrical advertise-
ments or critiques. During the Famine he was a joint secretary
of a relief fund raised in Belfast, working up to seven hours a
day on relief business, and in 1854 he became president of the
newly formed Christ Church protestant association, whose
objectives included the repeal of the catholic relief act of 1829.[31]

Again, in Dublin John Alcock, chaplain of Bethesda, showed
what could be done by systematic, and as regards himself,
unsparing, organization. On Monday there was a prayer
meeting; on Wednesday an expository lecture; on Thursday a
class for young men, which later developed into a branch of the
young men's christian association; on Friday a class for young

ladies, whose short essays Alcock carefully corrected and discussed. Members of this class supplied teachers for the Sunday schools attached to the church and two of them played a part in starting St Patrick's home for providing trained nurses for the poor. On Saturday Alcock worked on his sermons for Sunday – always carefully prepared and delivered extemporaneously. His feelings, it was said, were clothed in words which were 'simple, natural and well chosen', and he was able to express himself with 'a large measure of dramatic faculty'. 'His very finger', it was said, 'was full of eloquence.' It may be added that though Alcock declared, 'rarely do I, or can I, take up a book for amusement and not ever for relaxation', on occasion he read Shakespeare aloud with considerable effect.[32]

Further south, George Webster became rector of St Nicholas, Cork, in 1858. A man of great drive and a preacher whose wit and humour at times was 'a coruscation that leaped out with unexpected and ever startling flashes', he soon thoroughly organized his parish, which contained over 2,000 members of the Church of Ireland. There were frequent celebrations of holy communion. The interior of the church was remodelled, the organ being moved to the chancel and seats for a surpliced choir installed. A tower and steeple with a clock were erected (Webster securing subscriptions from Roman catholics on the grounds that it was of use to the general public). By 1865 there were in the parish the St Nicholas young men's society, which was studying Butler's *Analogy*, a Dorcas society for the relief of poor and industrious protestants, and a fellowship society to provide for the relief of distress, a library, a choir fund and six schools. Webster also played an active part in securing improved conditions for the sick in the north and south infirmaries (he advocated the introduction of nuns to nurse the Roman catholic patients), and in time started an industrial school for protestant boys and founded a hall of residence for Church of Ireland students at Queen's College, Cork. A fervent admirer of archbishop Whately and a man with great independence of mind, Webster almost inevitably became involved in controversy. As a young curate in Donnybrook in the 1850s, he played a prominent part in suppressing the famous and disorderly fair. Shortly after he arrived in Cork, a lecture he gave to the Cork young men's association, in which he argued that dancing and singing were not in themselves sinful, aroused hostile comment. He was a supporter of the national board's system of primary education, and he was a vehement opponent of the total-abstinence movement, 'as compromising the principle of Christian liberty, and substituting a rule of asceticism for the watchful and continual exercise of self-control'. He also thought that by adopting certain practices in public worship associated with high church opinions 'he could effectually deprive these observances of dogmatic significance' (a policy which could be misunderstood). A candid friend, dean Dickinson, who greatly admired Webster's robust integrity, regretted that owing to his liberal attitude on both ecclesiastical and political questions, Webster never had an opportunity of playing a leading and influential part in the councils of the church (he was never elected to the general synod and only once to the Cork diocesan council). As a result, Dickinson thought, Webster's energies were enervated by the atmosphere of 'provincialism and parochialism' in which he worked, and his time was wasted on 'questions of little or no importance outside the city and diocese'. But then Dickinson was, during all his ecclesiastical career, a metropolitan clergyman.[33]

A country clergyman, too, could be kept busy. The curate of Offerlane, in the diocese of Ossory, a parish covering about 50,000 acres with 800 Church of Ireland parishioners, explained in a letter to his bishop that there were four 'scriptural schools' in the parish, in each of which he taught for two hours every week. In addition there were twelve places at which during the week he gave catechetical instruction to families which lived miles from a school or who were 'of a rank superior to that by which the schools are used'. When he considered the amount of pastoral visiting he did on foot, he was indignant at 'sleek M.P.s. talking of idle drones'.[34]

The curate of Offerlane's reference to his schools is a reminder that in a large number of parishes the incumbent managed and supported or tried to obtain support for a primary school or schools. Education in nineteenth-century Ireland was regarded as a panacea for many ills and was also a complex and contro-versial subject. From the beginning of the century voluntary societies, often dominated by members of the established church, were at work providing facilities for primary education. In

1831 the government set up the national board, to supervise and subsidize schools conducted on the principle of united secular and separate religious instruction. Many members of the establishment were unable to accept the system and in 1839 the church education society was founded to assist schools staffed by Church of Ireland teachers. In these schools, along with secular education, scriptural education based on the authorized version was provided for all children attending, and the Church of Ireland pupils received instruction in the catechism and formularies of their church. At first the church education society was supported by 'almost the whole of the rank and influence of the church, at a time when outside the church there was little of individual rank or influence anywhere'. In 1867 the church education society was helping about 1,400 schools with about 63,000 children on their rolls of whom 44,000 were episcopalians.[35] But the society was feeling the strain of competing with a state-supported system. As early as 1850 it had to be admitted that its teachers were more poorly paid than those in the national schools, and by 1870 it also had to be admitted that standards in the society's schools were below those in the national schools. Moreover, from the outset, opinion in the church was divided on the educational question. There were those who held that it was permissible for Church of Ireland-managed primary schools to be associated with the board, and this opinion gained ground when it was realized that the bulk of the schools tended to be denominational schools with pupils from a minority group protected by a conscience clause. The change of opinion was shown in 1866 when the primate, five bishops and over 700 clergymen subscribed to a declaration stating that they favoured united secular education and approved in general of the national board system. After 1870 the church education society declined in importance, 'deserted', as it complained 'by very many especially in high places'. The number of schools it assisted had fallen to 138 by 1900. On the other hand, by the beginning of the new century there were 1,330 schools under Church of Ireland management in the national board system. By then the Church of Ireland had under its control a training college for primary school teachers, the Kildare Place training college. This college had been started in Kildare Place in 1814 by the church education society and when the society was no longer able to maintain it, it was taken over in 1878 by the education committee appointed by the general synod.[36]

It should be added that, besides the primary schools supported by members of the Church of Ireland, there were under episcopalian control over thirty schools, a few of which might have been regarded as the Irish equivalent of an English public school, the rest being grammar schools. Many of the latter were small and badly managed, but the former group included the four successful royal schools, Armagh, Dungannon, Enniskillen and Raphoe and St Columba's College, Rathfarnham, which had been founded by a group of Irishmen inspired by the Oxford movement to provide an education 'in strict accordance with the principles and formularies of the established church' on English public school lines.

The church education society was the most prominent society associated with the Church of Ireland in the pre-disestablishment era. But there were many other societies – *Thom's Directory* lists at least thirty which called on the members of the church for support and which afforded an outlet for their religious feelings and their benevolent and administrative energies. Some of these were anglican societies, for instance the CMS, the SPCK, the SPG, the additional curates' fund, the incorporated society for protestant schools, the scripture readers' society. Others, though they received support from protestants of other denominations, were largely managed by members of the established church, for instance the national association for the education of the deaf and dumb children of the poor, the Hibernian Bible society, the protestant orphan society.

These societies were a sign of religious vitality, and even a harsh critic of the establishment, James Godkin in *Ireland and her churches*, which appeared in 1867, admitted that in the past thirty years there had been 'a great increase of life in the Irish church', though he was quick to add that this had resulted from what might be called the formation within the establishment of a voluntary church based on the religious societies and proprietary chapels. On the whole, however, Godkin's picture of the Church of Ireland, compounded of statistics, unsympathetic observation and hostile anecdotage, was unfavourable. He dwelt forcibly on episcopal wealth, nepotism and hauteur,

on clerical indolence and absenteeism, on the anomalies created
by the historic parochial system, on the disparities between
duties and incomes, and 'on the passion for territory irrespective
of population' which he thought characteristic of a church
which prided itself on making provision for its ministrations in
every corner of Ireland.[37] The year before Godkin published his
philippic against the establishment, a young Scottish episcopalian clergyman, MacColl, an acquaintance and admirer of
Gladstone, when on a short visit to Ireland, received a most
unfavourable impression of the established church. Staying in
Westmeath, he went on Sunday to the local parish church and
afterwards he wrote:[38]

A more melancholy sight I never beheld. The congregation consisted
of five county families who spend the season in London; so that the
congregation must consist in the summer of the incumbent's family.
There were no poor, and I never saw so undevotional a congregation.
During the prayers no one knelt. Some stood with their backs to the
altar and the officiating clergyman, and one knee resting on the seat,
some sat and others reclined in the half empty pews nursing one leg
stretched out full length on the cushioned seat. During the singing no
more than half the congregation stood up and the same during the
reading of the gospel. The more I see of the Irish church, the more I
feel there is no life in it; and that it is simply cumbering the ground.

Godkin, as a presbyterian, had an instinctive dislike for a
hierarchical and endowed church; as a nineteenth-century
liberal, he was quick to detect and resent the misapplication of
what he regarded as public funds; and he considered the
Church of Ireland's status as an establishment an embittering
factor in Irish politics. As for MacColl, a combative high
churchman, he possibly exaggerated the significance of the
non-observance of rules of behaviour which had become
prevalent in England comparatively recently.

Forty years after Godkin and MacColl recorded their
criticisms, William Alexander, appointed bishop of Derry in
1867, tried to assess the worth of the established church in
which he had been born and in which he had worked for almost
a quarter of a century. 'Let me' he wrote in 1905[39]

say something about certain salient merits and defects of the pre-
Disestablishment Church. First, its merits. As regards externals, the
churches of the dreary architecture of the long-departed and little-

lamented ecclesiastical commissioners are scarcely capable of finding a name. They were scarcely edifices or structures, though in a
certain limited sense they were possibly buildings. The services were,
apparently, at least to strangers, somewhat frigid. Neither clergy nor
people had found that the liturgy had lips of fire, that discovery cost
the Church of England, as well as gave it, a good deal. In Ireland
the discovery has cost us nothing, because the excess called ritualism
is impossible. But let us note this: the evangelical revival in Ireland
was wonderful and it was almost everywhere. If we had a process of
beatification, I could point to signs of sainthood not to be denied by
those by whom they were seen. Now, as for the work of the clergy; no
doubt there were more parishes than there are at present where the
incumbents were lax; but this was in many cases partly made up for
by excellent and zealous curates. There was little machinery or
organization; and many departments of Christian work were scarcely
discovered. But Sunday schools were carried on with an enthusiasm
which was sometimes astonishing. Missionary meetings had the
charm of novelty and were largely attended. Preaching was warm
hearted and simple, often extemporaneous. The sermons might have
little of the antithesis which is the masculine affectation of strength,
or of the imagery which is feminine affectation of beauty; but they
were as a general rule earnest and simple, and few of that description
which a much-loved bishop described as 'not having enough gospel
to save a tit-mouse'. Above all parochial visitation was carried out
with a regularity and determination which reminded one of Saint
Paul's great utterance – 'warning every man and teaching every
man, we may present every man perfect in Christ'. The appointment
to parishes was mostly in the hands of bishops. No doubt there was
too much room during many years for the imputation of nepotism.
But I must take care not to speak too long or too partially. For me
the old established church lies in deep and tender distances. Unforgotten faces and unforgotten graves present themselves to memory.
Young people were brought up to believe that the relation between
Church and State could not be broken without a lowered moral
atmosphere, as well as peril to protestantism. Many pronounced the
words 'church and state' not as men shout them in their cups but as
they breathe them in their prayers.

Alexander's words bring forcibly home what the Church of
Ireland could mean to a man of great sensitivity and goodness,
who was aware that it had defects and limitations, but was
nevertheless profoundly conscious of its virtues and its value
both to its own members and to the community as a whole.

II

DISESTABLISHMENT

~~~~~~

AS HAS BEEN already pointed out, the Church of Ireland at the beginning of the nineteenth century suffered from the obvious weakness that its adherents amounted to barely an eighth of the population. In the eighteenth century, an age favourable to establishments, Paley had firmly pronounced that 'efficacy' required that the magistrate, when he was choosing the religion to be established, should take into account the faith of the nation rather than his own beliefs. Of course, when it was widely held that only a member of the established church was a full citizen, the numerical weakness of the Irish establishment could be ignored, and during a conservative age in a contented country, the Irish branch of the establishment might have survived as a tolerated anomaly. But Ireland was not a contented country, and after catholic emancipation the growing social and economic power of the catholic community, together with the strength of utilitarianism in British politics, threatened the position of the Irish establishment. In the early thirties, even before the debates on the great reform bill had ended, the privileges of the established church in both England and Ireland were being vigorously denounced. Needless to say, the assailants concentrated their attacks on the weaker branch, the Church of Ireland. Liberals, radicals and repealers challenged its right to its status and to its endowments; and over much of the south and west of Ireland during the early 1830s there was a well-organized general strike in opposition to the payment of tithe. In the end the establishment weathered the storm. Fortunately for the Church of Ireland the whig governments which were in power during the 1830s, while anxious to restore order in Ireland by fair play and practical reforms, were reluctant to embark on radical reconstruction or to make sweeping constitutional changes. The Irish establishment was probably strengthened by two major whig measures which were both strenuously resisted by Irish churchmen, the ecclesiastical temporalities act of 1833, and the tithe commutation act of 1838. The ecclesiastical temporalities act to a limited degree rationalized the distribution of the church's revenues by providing for the uniting of dioceses and by setting up an ecclesiastical commission empowered to divide parishes, tax the better endowed incumbencies and subsidize poorer livings. The tithe act transferred the obligation to pay tithe from the occupier to the landlord. And from about 1840 the Church of Ireland enjoyed a quarter of a century of comparative security. Ireland was exhausted by the Famine and Irish nationalists were dispirited and disorganized. In British politics the 1850s and 1860s were 'an era of good-feeling', symbolized by the ascendancy of Palmerston, a liberal prime minister with deeply ingrained conservative instincts.

Even so, the Irish church question was not completely dormant. Advanced liberals in Great Britain continued to believe that the maintenance of the Church of Ireland as an established church in Ireland was 'at the root of the evils of that country'.[1] In Ireland, the leaders, clerical and lay, of the post-emancipation generation of catholics, were becoming increasingly insistent that the principles of religious or denominational equality should prevail in all spheres. Tending to view resentfully those privileges, the product of centuries of power still enjoyed by protestants, they urged with increasing emphasis that the Church of Ireland, whose status was a reminder of an unhappy past, should be disestablished.

In 1854 William Shee, MP for county Kilkenny, urged that a portion of the revenues of the Church of Ireland should be diverted to the catholic and presbyterian churches in Ireland. Two years later, Miall, the leading liberationist, introduced a motion attacking all ecclesiastical endowments in Ireland, and in 1863 and 1865 Dillyn and Bernal Osborne both raised the question of religious endowments in Ireland, making considerable play with the results of the 1861 census; and in 1865 Dillyn introduced a motion to the effect that the position of the establishment in Ireland was unsatisfactory. Though these attacks were all repelled, the critics of the establishment mustered a fair amount of parliamentary support and it was noticeable that in the 1865 debates Gladstone, the chancellor of the exchequer, though he opposed Dillyn's motion on the grounds that the government was not prepared to deal with the question, ominously declared that he considered the present state of the Irish church establishment to be unsatisfactory.[2]

It was also ominous that the conservative leader in the house of commons, Disraeli (who twenty years before had referred to the Church of Ireland as 'an alien church'), did not speak in the debates on Dillyn's motions. On both occasions he was urged to do so by a leading Irish conservative, Joseph Napier, an ex-lord chancellor of Ireland and a fervent evangelical churchman. In 1865 Napier suggested to Disraeli that it was desirable that the debate on Dillyn's motion 'should be not dealt with as a mere Irish squabble about the Irish church but on its true merits as a movement of dissent and democracy against a religious establishment and a landed gentry'. And he strove to impress on the conservative leader his belief that 'you cannot have English government here without the established church'. It is only fair to add that Napier did not rely merely on a stone-walling defence of the church's position. He wanted[3]

to soften the antagonism of the churches by encouraging toleration and co-operation, to make the members of the United Church better churchmen and better Irishmen, with less polemical bitterness and less of puritan exclusiveness; to make the Roman Catholics less papal and less ultramontane and more truly national and legal.

Napier was public-spirited and well meaning but his conception of co-operation would clearly have left the Church of Ireland's status unimpaired.

The spokesmen of the Irish establishment, as might be expected, remained remarkably unshaken by the attacks on their church. They denounced the 'rhetorical exaggerations' and 'falsifications of statistical returns' indulged in by critics of the church.[4] Mere numbers, it was pointed out, were not everything. 'A church', Beresford of Armagh, declared:[5]

that embraces so large a proportion of the educated classes, which numbers among its members the inheritors of the great historic names of the country, a majority of the learned professions, and the mercantile classes, and which has implanted the principles of industry, order and loyalty for which the protestant population is so remarkable, cannot be said to have failed in its mission.

Lifting the debate to a high level, the defenders of the establishment argued that it was the duty of the state to support religious truth. 'We cannot contemplate without trembling for the consequences', Bernard, the bishop of Tuam, wrote, 'the bare idea of a great nation which has pledged itself to the maintenance of evangelicalism and protestant truth, falsifying pledges.'[6] Lee, the warm-tempered and learned archdeacon of Dublin, referred scornfully to those speculative politicians who would 'deal with the worship of God as with a question of free trade'.[7] And Magee, the dean of Cork, a man of tremendous energy, who combined a strong independent intellect with a great sense of humour and a quick, stimulating (and at times dangerous) wit, argued, in an important article in the *Contemporary Review*, that the Church of Ireland was a truly national church because, he wrote, 'it asserts the idea of a free national life against the anti-national despotism of the papacy'. The Church of Ireland, Magee contended, was not a creation of the English crown. Henry II on coming to Ireland had found it 'already an established and endowed church' and it accepted the English monarch as ruler of Ireland. The 'Anglo-Celtic' church as Magee termed it had had its failures. During the middle ages it failed to make a united nation of the Anglo-Irish and the Celts. And at the time of the reformation it did not convert the Celtic section of the population. But it had 'preserved loyalty, religion and civilization amongst the Anglo-Celts' and was a witness for 'a purer faith and a nobler national life against ultramontane despotism'. It should be added that, writing to a friend a few months before his article appeared, Magee put part of his argument more bluntly:[8]

In spite of all Dr Lee and Stopford may take out of old records to prove that ecclesiastically we are the national church of Ireland, the established church never has been since the reformation, or long before it, the church of the nation. It has been all along the church of the Pale and the church of Anglo-Celtic colony in Ireland.

29

It was, however, suggested that the establishment should try and reorganize its resources so as to be able to show that they were not excessive and were being utilized efficiently. In 1863, Stopford, the archdeacon of Meath, and an expert on ecclesiastical law, warned some leading conservatives that if the question of the Irish church was not settled under Palmerston, it would be used as the one question on which all sections of the liberal party could unite. A few years later Stopford optimistically suggested that 'territorial rearrangements would go far to remove anomalies', and at the beginning of 1864 the Irish bishops prepared a bill which would have dissolved seventeen cathedral chapters and provided a simplified procedure for the unification and division of benefices. But the government informed the bishops that it was not prepared to sponsor the bill and during the following session, with a general election impending, the bishop thought it would be injudicious to introduce it.[9] It was significant that at the general election of 1865 one of the candidates for the university constituency, John Ball, the vicar-general for the diocese of Armagh, emphasized in his election address how urgently important it was for the Church of Ireland to secure the legislation required 'for the improvement of the laws regulating her internal economy and polity'. Ball, an able lawyer, deeply attached to the church, pointed out that he possessed considerable expertise on ecclesiastical questions, but he also announced that he was a liberal, at least to the extent of supporting Palmerston, and the university constituency rejected him in favour of a strong conservative.

Attempts were also made to provide institutional machinery through which the church could express its views effectively. In 1860 the Irish archbishop and bishops, having reminded the government that the convocations of Canterbury and York had been licensed to discuss canon twenty-nine, requested that before any changes in doctrine or discipline should be made, 'the advice of a general synod of the United Church of England and Ireland' should be obtained. The Irish church, Fitzgerald, the bishop of Cork, argued at this time, should have 'a fair share in a general convocation of the united church'. 'The true policy of empire', he declared, required 'the most intimate possible blending of all parts of that empire.' But a whig government was not sympathetic to ecclesiastical experiments, and it refused to summon a 'general synod of the United Church' or license for business a meeting of convocation in Ireland.[10] Some years later, when the debate on disestablishment was gathering strength, a vigorous group of Church of Ireland clergymen led by Magee, the dean of Cork, wanted the Irish archbishops to hold meetings of their provincial synods (it was in fact customary for the archbishop of Dublin to summon regularly a meeting of the provincial synods of Dublin and Tuam, but it met only *pro forma*). But the law officers of the crown held that the act of Henry VIII embodying the submission of the clergy (25 Henry VIII c. 19), being declaratory of the common law, applied to Ireland, and that provincial synods were ecclesiastical assemblies which could only meet with the crown's permission. For good measure they added that the Irish convention act of 1793 (aimed at radical gatherings) also forbade such assemblies.[11] The archbishops deferred to the law officers' opinion and refrained from summoning the synods. But it should be recorded that by the beginning of the 1860s one bishop, Knox of Down and Connor and Dromore, was holding an annual meeting of his clergy at which papers on church questions were read and discussed. Moreover, Knox welcomed at these gatherings 'such of the laity as were introduced by the clergy' and in 1863 he expressed the wish that each parish should be represented at the meeting by a layman selected by the incumbent. Laymen played an active part in the discussions and, at the meeting in 1865, Reichel declared that if diocesan synods were revived they should include lay representatives.[12]

The general election of 1865, which strengthened the more advanced section of the liberal party, was followed by the death of Palmerston, who was succeeded by Russell as prime minister. These events marked the beginning of a new era when Victorian liberalism was again on the march. And just about the time the Russell cabinet was formed, a series of arrests and trials revealed the extent and determination of the Fenian movement, a movement which expressed Irish discontent in an extreme and violent form. No British politician was prepared to yield to Fenianism. But common sense dictated that efforts should immediately be made to weaken the power of extreme nationalism by conciliating responsible catholic opinion – which for some time had been demanding disestablishment.

However, the supporters of the Irish church were heartened when in June the manoeuvrings over parliamentary reform brought the conservatives into office. But the conservative government, led by Lord Derby until he was replaced by Disraeli in February 1868, relied on a minority in the house of commons and, anxious to acquire parliamentary and public support, it showed itself to be remarkably flexible on political issues. In May 1867 Naas, the chief secretary, enunciated that to take away the property of the Church of Ireland would be confiscation; in June the government accepted a motion of Russell's demanding the appointment of a commission to inquire into the revenues of the established Church of Ireland, and in March 1868 the chief secretary, while deploring the suggestion that there should be a levelling down of ecclesiastical endowments in Ireland, declared that justice might demand a greater equalization of endowments than then existed.[13]

If the conservatives in the spring of 1868 were cautious about committing themselves to the defence of the Irish branch of the establishment, the attitude of the liberal party was clearly defined when on 30 March Gladstone moved that the house of commons should go into committee to consider the acts relating to the Irish church. Thirty years earlier, Gladstone, then 'the rising hope of the stern, unbending tories', in his *The state in its relation with the church*, a serious and sustained exposition of the traditional theory of the alliance between church and state, had defended the maintenance of the establishment in Ireland on the highest grounds. 'It appears not too much to assume', he wrote, 'that our imperial legislature had been qualified to take and has taken, in fact, a sounder view of religious truth than the majority of Ireland in their destitute and uninstructed state.' Naturally his conspicuous change of opinion on the Irish church question attracted bitter attention and was strongly attacked. Disraeli, not Gladstone's most charitable critic, attributed Gladstone's attack on the Irish church to his determination to become prime minister. 'Strange', Disraeli wrote, 'that a desire to create bishops should lead a man to destroy churches.' Even Wilberforce, the bishop of Oxford, Gladstone's friend and fervent admirer, was momentarily critical. In March 1868, he thought that Gladstone was influenced by 'his restlessness at being out of office' and by 'his hatred to the low tone of the Irish branch'.[14] Gladstone himself at the close of 1868 published a forceful apologia. In *A fragment of autobiography*, he admits his change of opinion on the Irish church question. But he emphasizes that it was a slow and deliberate process, forced on him by changing circumstances, political, social and religious. He was profoundly thankful that the United Kingdom was still a Christian community. But he could not agree that an established church, supported by a very small minority of the population, was the best means of upholding Christian truth in Ireland.

In his speech on 30 March Gladstone declared himself in favour of terminating the connection between the Church of Ireland and the state. Disestablishment was to be accompanied by disendowment. But vested interests were to be respected and, Gladstone emphasized, 'every disposition should exist to indulge and to conciliate feeling when it could be done, and in every doubtful case to adopt that mode of proceeding which may be most consistent with principles of the largest equity'.[15] The cabinet seems to have been divided and uncertain over what its attitude should be in the long term to the Irish church question. One minister at least was playing with the idea of 'disestablishment without disendowment'. Disraeli himself thought that the conservative case should be that 'the whole question of national establishments is now raised'. But, he added, 'we must detach the Irish church as much as possible from the prominent position of the subject for there is no doubt it is not popular'.[16] Understandably then, the government did not meet Gladstone's motion with a complete negative: instead, it proposed an amendment to the effect that the Irish church question should be reserved for the decision of the new parliament. Stanley, the government's spokesman in a speech which Cairns characterized as 'colourless and chilling',[17] while criticizing Gladstone's approach, carefully avoided giving any indication of what was going to be the conservatives' policy. But Gladstone had raised an issue which united all sections of the liberal party, a party which had been sorely divided in the recent debates on parliamentary reform. Moreover, he was suggesting a remedy for Irish discontent, which had become such a disturbing problem in British politics. And his motion was carried by 333 votes to 270. In April, by even larger majorities, the house of commons agreed to a series of resolutions embodying his policy and a suspensory bill suspending all appointments to vacant benefices in the gift of the crown was carried through the house of commons in the teeth of the government. This bill was defeated in the lords and the government did not resign, but it was clearly understood that there would be a general election in the near future.

The divisions of opinion among English churchmen at this time on the Irish church question were reflected at a great meeting, held under the chairmanship of the archbishop of Canterbury (Longley) at St James's Hall, to condemn Gladstone's proposals. Napier was extremely pleased at securing as speakers Wilberforce, generally considered a high churchman, and Stanley, a leading broad churchman, in spite of the 'narrow minded feelings of many'. Wilberforce, who was greeted with hisses by a section of the audience whom he called 'sibilant geese', in an eloquent speech declared that the object of an establishment was 'to raise the whole department of government from the low Dogberry and Verges level up to the intimation of the Almighty's will'; and, he emphasized, it was the duty of a nation to establish what it believed to be the true form of worship. The bishop of London, Tait, spoke in a lower key. To him the establishment seemed to be a check on clerical presumption and eccentricity. A disestablished church, he said, would be 'in my estimation a church not free but given to licence'. Stanley, who argued that the connection between church and state could not be maintained in Ireland unless great changes were made, was shouted down.[18]

In September 1868 the report of the commission of inquiry into the established Church of Ireland was published. It recommended a further consolidation of dioceses (reducing the episcopate to one archbishop and seven bishops), a considerable reorganization of parishes and a redistribution of clerical incomes. Though the commission did not suggest that there should be a measure of disendowment, obviously such a drastic overhaul of the church's finances was bound to involve dangerous implications, and leading churchmen were afraid the government would go beyond the commission's recommendations. Trench, as early as April 1868, was sure Disraeli would propose a scheme for a 'starved and cut-down establishment which will leave all causes of irritation existing still', and which 'being a compromise resting on no intelligent principle will inevitably cease to exist after a few years'. Trench's own policy was simply 'to fight for everything we possess as believing it rightfully ours'. If defeated, he preferred 'instant death' at the hands of Gladstone to Disraeli's 'gradual starvation'. Magee of Cork, who regarded the conservative and liberal leaders as 'rival solicitors ... bidding for the carriage of our sale', characterized the conservatives' Irish church policy as 'death by repeated bleedings'.[19]

At the close of the year 1868 the newly enlarged electorate was asked to decide between the two great parties. Both the party leaders, Disraeli and Gladstone, emphasized the significance of the Irish church question. Disestablishment was to Gladstone 'the discharge of a debt of civil justice'. To Disraeli the connection of religion with political authority was 'one of the main safeguards of the civilization of man'. Disraeli sensed that a great upsurge of protestant feeling was rising which he hoped would benefit the conservatives at the polls. But not being in close touch with contemporary religious currents, he seems to have over-estimated the extent to which protestant feeling would express itself in voting conservative – after all there were strong, well-tested links between liberalism and protestant dissent, and some high churchmen had become disillusioned with political conservatism. In August, when discussing election tactics. Disraeli saw as a desideratum, 'a good protestant appointment in the church'. He had been 'expecting a bishop to die every day' but in default of an episcopal vacancy he decided, as a significant gesture, to appoint to the deanery of Ripon Hugh MacNeile, an Antrim man and a Trinity, Dublin, graduate, who was a well-known evangelical preacher. Ten years earlier Napier had urged that MacNeile, 'so steadfast, so good a man, who has never wavered in the cause of the protestant religion and the liberties of England', should be given preferment. The queen however complained that moderate men did not like MacNeile's promotion. Disraeli replied assuring her that MacNeile's appointment to what was after all only 'a mock deanery', had satisfied 'some millions of Your

Majesty's subjects', and given the crown more latitude when the time came to fill a vacant bishopric. This eventuality occurred shortly after MacNeile's appointment on the death of the bishop of Peterborough. Disraeli's first candidate was in the queen's opinion an 'insignificant low churchman', and she suggested instead Magee 'the distinguished dean of Cork'. Disraeli was surprised but reacted favourably when he realized that Magee's appointment would 'prove our recognition of the unity of the church, colonial and Irish etc.' (Though he saw one objection to Magee's promotion, 'it would give us nothing'.) Thus Magee escaped from Ireland. Five years' experience had destroyed his hope of 'raising a standard of liberality and moderation' there. 'Tory politics and "gospel" theology', he wrote 'will sway the Irish church for at least one generation.'[20]

But though both Disraeli and Gladstone laid great emphasis on the Irish church question, they each put other issues in the forefront, and even a cursory survey of the general election at constituency level shows what a variety of questions, national and local, were brought before the voters during the election. The result was a large liberal majority. Disraeli at once re-signed, and Gladstone, immediately after becoming prime minister, took steps to prepare a measure dealing with the Irish church. He was convinced that if civil and religious equality were to be accepted as governing principles in British politics, the established church in Ireland must lose its privileges. But as a devout Christian and a loyal anglican, he was deeply concerned for the future of the Church of Ireland. As he himself wrote, a quarter of a century later:

In approaching the question of Irish disestablishment my leading idea was this – we were about to carry the established church of Ireland out of an existence defined by statutory conditions into one purely voluntary and severed from state authority. Our duty, as it appeared to me was this: to make that severance complete and to take care that we did not lacerate or in any way impair the means of action belonging to her as a church or religious society and leave her like any other religious society to any and every claims she might consider herself to possess on other than statutory grounds.

Moreover, Gladstone was sure that after disestablishment on the lines he proposed, 'the new religious body will commence its new form of existence with much of the property as well as much of the undefined important social credit that had belonged to the old one'.[21]

Naturally then, Gladstone was anxious to discuss his measure with leading Irish churchmen. As an experienced politician, he could not be oblivious to the advantages of securing a substantial degree of agreement on a highly contentious bill. But his primary concern seems to have been to see how far he could meet the wishes of the leaders of the Church of Ireland on points of detail, while, of course, adhering to the broad principles of his plan. For a moment it seemed possible that the government might be able to open negotiations with a body representing the Irish church. Shortly after the election the Irish bishops, anxious that the government (and the country at large) should have an opportunity of hearing the opinions of Irish churchmen, again requested permission for a meeting of convocation in Ireland. Gladstone intimated that the government might consider allowing convocation to meet if it were agreed that the assembly would, under protest if it so desired, accept the government's plan as a basis for discussion. But understandably the government was not prepared to give legal sanction to an assembly set on opposing its policy. The bishops did not respond to Gladstone's suggestion and permission for a meeting of convocation was not granted.

In December Gladstone tried to open negotiations with the archbishop of Dublin, but Trench was not encouraging. He seems to have considered that an invitation to discuss with the government a bill, based on the principle 'that everything shall be taken away from us that can be taken away' was 'a superfluous mockery', and he later compared the leaders of the Church of Ireland to 'the garrison of a hard pressed city' invited 'to assist at a conference by which they were to be put to the sword'.[22] The archbishop, however, allowed his views to reach Gladstone indirectly through an eminent liberal lawyer, Roundell Palmer, who had refused the lord chancellorship at the end of 1868 because he could not consciously support disestablishment. In January 1869 Palmer visited Dublin and, during a long after-dinner talk, the archbishop told him that it was impossible for the bishops to speak for the Irish clergy and laity when convocation was not permitted to meet. 'It would never do', the archbishop went on to say, for Gladstone to be able to get up in the house of commons and say he had come to terms with the Irish clergy. It would be ruin to the clergy in the estimation of the conservative party and in the estimation of the laity of the Irish establishment.

The archbishop hoped that the government would be forced to grant reasonable terms to the church by the difficulties which would be created by differences in the liberal party, by the action of the house of lords and by the pressure of public opinion. 'I rely', he declared, 'on the justice of the English people. They will not see us stripped of our just rights.' After a dinner with the archbishop in London, Palmer was able to present to the prime minister a memorandum in which he set out the terms on which he gathered leading churchmen in Ireland considered they could advise their people to accept or at least acquiesce in the government's measure. These were briefly that the disestablished church would retain the churches and glebe houses and parochial endowments granted since the reformation, that the life interests of present incumbents would be respected and that the church would be left free to arrange its future form of government. Palmer did not receive an answer from Gladstone, which, he later noted, was just as well, since[23]

Archbishop Trench found it difficult to bring those whom he consulted in Ireland to the point which would have been necessary for any sort of understanding with the government; and told me . . . that he was anxious that Gladstone should not give them any answer good or bad.

Trench, who was at this time afraid of the Irish laity and distrustful of the English conservative leaders (whom he suspected of being ready to use the Irish church as a pawn in their political battles), was obviously dismayed at the prospect of becoming entangled in negotiations with Gladstone, a master of political dialectics. Gladstone however managed to establish fruitful relations with a more robust Irish churchman, Edward Stopford, archdeacon of Meath, the author of a standard work on Irish ecclesiastical law. Stopford had fought vigorously for the maintenance of the establishment, but after the general election of 1868 he accepted what seemed to be the inevitable and prepared to do his best to render the transition as smooth as possible – even at the cost of collaborating with a liberal

government. A few weeks after Gladstone took office Stopford
wrote to him saying:[24]

Opposed as I am on principle to the disestablishment of the church
in Ireland to which I can be no party [I am ready] to accept the
inevitable and to withdraw the Church of Ireland from the arena of
party conflict by accepting a measure of disestablishment in this
session of parliament.

And he offered to assist Gladstone in drafting his bill. Gladstone
invited the archdeacon to Hawarden and was much impressed
by his ability and knowledge. Stopford, who in his relations
with the prime minister showed dignified independence of
spirit, approached the technical problems created by disestablishment from the standpoint of an expert on canon law
and a loyal member of the church. As he himself wrote, 'verbal
differences may have a great effect. I have great experience in
drawing bills with able lawyers. They never see how they touch
bishops. I do.' Stopford also provided the prime minister with
material for a paradox. 'It is a curious thing', Gladstone
remarked years later, 'that the two most laconic men I ever
met were Irishmen, Parnell and Archdeacon Stopford.'[25]

Stopford was able to influence the shaping of the bill: for
instance he favoured 1871 as the date for disestablishment
becoming operative and he pressed for a generous settlement of
the glebe house question and a provision which would permit
'compounding' by the clergy. Early in 1869 he seems to have
hoped that a group of Church of Ireland clergymen might be
formed which would issue a public pronouncement in favour
of accepting the result of the general election. Gladstone, when
he heard of this project, was much impressed with 'the great
advantage of establishing a party of concession in Ireland',
which would help to remove 'the most formidable stumbling
block in our way', the house of lords. The Irish attorney general,
Sullivan, was discouraging. He told Gladstone that few Irish
churchmen had much foresight and that 'Stopford has no
following'. Stopford himself, on returning to Ireland at the end
of January, was amazed at the amount of support he received.
But he had to add that 'the men who would now come forward
openly with me are too few . . . and they fear awaking suspicion
in the laity'.[26]

39

There were, of course, members of the Church of Ireland who supported or at least acquiesced in Gladstone's policy. Maziere Brady, a county Meath incumbent and an industrious ecclesiastical antiquarian, proclaimed in print that what he termed the English state church in Ireland was heavily over-endowed. Brady, whose views were unusual in a clergyman of the establishment, subsequently became a Roman catholic and was appointed an assistant librarian in the Vatican. A few more conventional churchmen, Knox, the bishop of Down, Atkins, the dean of Ferns, and MacDonnell, the dean of Cashel, all intimated to Gladstone that they would not oppose his policy. The bishop of Down was convinced that nothing was more foolish 'than a mere defiant and idle cry of "No surrender"',[27] and MacDonnell's old friend Magee, now bishop of Peterborough, was convinced after the general election that disestablishment was inevitable. 'The battle this year', he wrote at the beginning of 1869, would be 'one of amendments not of field days and resolutions.' Magee was anxious to prevent the Irish tories using the Irish church for their own political ends, and he thought that the best plan would be for the English bishops to save the dignity of the Irish bench by 'advising their Irish brethren to compromise'. But he saw clearly the awkward problems involved in attempting to implement a compromise between the Church of Ireland and the government. 'We are in the position', he wrote,[28]

of a garrison besieged by a hostile army, half regular, half savages. Is Gladstone strong enough to keep his savages from scalping us if we lay down our arms? On the other hand, he may say, are you strong enough to ensure me the surrender of the fortress if I disband and disarm my savages. . . . Neither side can guarantee its engagements.

At a bishops' meeting held at Lambeth on 10 February 1869, Magee – who had had a talk with Gladstone – argued that 'the time was come when the Irish church could get more by compromise than by fight'. The Irish bishops, who were at the meeting, made it pathetically plain that, though they were not optimistic about the outcome of the struggle, they had to reckon on 'the jealously watchful laity', and the primate (according to Magee) concluded by stressing 'that he would not regard anything as inevitable . . . and finally wandered and

fairly maundered in a feeble way that was most painful'.[29]
Before this meeting Gladstone had met Magee, and a week after
it he had a meeting with Tait, the new archbishop of Canterbury. Tait, who had an aptitude for politics, was reluctant to
throw the Church of England athwart public opinion in a
doubtful cause. When he met Gladstone on 19 February, the
interview 'took the form of an exposition of his policy by Mr
Gladstone'. This exposition on the whole reassured the archbishop. The continuance of the Church of Ireland as a legal
entity was to be provided for, life interests were to be calculated
on a generous basis and it would be easy for the disestablished
church to retain its glebes and glebe houses. From then onwards
Tait was convinced that the best course was to take disestablishment for granted and to concentrate on obtaining the best
terms possible in the ultimate settlement. After disestablishment
'we will practically have in Ireland', he wrote, 'a branch of the
English established church. We should see that body is as
powerful and as wealthy as possible.'[30] Another prelate whom
Gladstone persuaded to accept Irish disestablishment as
inevitable was Wilberforce, the politic and influential bishop of
Oxford. Wilberforce met Gladstone at Hatfield about the middle
of December 1868 and found him 'as ever, great, earnest and
honest'. 'When people talk of Gladstone going mad', Wilberforce wrote, 'they do not take into account the great elasticity
of his mind and the variety of his interests.' Gladstone gathered
from Wilberforce's conversation that his attitude would be
'co-operation under protest'. Gladstone wrote to him pointing
out the value of English episcopal support for the bill.
Wilberforce agreed that this support would 'tear the heart of
opposition' and suggested terms for disestablishment not
significantly different from those which Gladstone was to
propose. Gladstone was justifiably pleased at having 'the bishop
of Oxford right on the Irish church'. In addition to his own
efforts Gladstone had persuaded 'two old friends to write to
him . . . of course not in my name'.[31]

The attitude of the English bench on the Irish church
question was shown when at the end of February, a week
before Gladstone introduced his bill, the convocation of
Canterbury met. The lower house inserted in the address to the
queen, prepared by the bishops, an amendment to the effect

that disestablishment 'cannot be had without repudiation on the part of this nation of the necessity and value of the reformation', and asked the upper house to join in a request to the queen not to assent to an Irish disestablishment bill. The upper house rejected both the request and the amendment and an address was adopted which simply expressed the deep anxiety of convocation respecting the proceedings in parliament relating to the Irish church and its hope that whatever received parliamentary sanction would tend to 'the peace and enlightenment and good government of Ireland'.[32]

While Gladstone was busy in consultation with some of his colleagues, and as far as possible with leading churchmen, drafting his Irish church bill, the leaders of the Church of Ireland, with very few exceptions, were bracing themselves for what might have seemed an almost hopeless struggle against a strong government, with a large majority in a new parliament. At the beginning of November 1868 a group of influential laymen, meeting in Dublin at the provost's house, had formed a consultative committee to co-operate with the bishops in opposing disestablishment. At the beginning of March 1869 this body approved of a scheme drafted by a sub-committee, providing for the representation of lay opinion. Parishes were to appoint lay delegates which were to meet in diocesan synods which would elect representatives to a general synod or conference of the Church of Ireland.[33] The first reaction of the primate to this plan was unfavourable. It seemed, he wrote, 'to take for granted that which we may hope to avoid'. Napier disapproved of the scheme on the grounds that to convene an assembly purporting to represent any description of the people was a violation of the convention act. 'Loyal men', he wrote, 'should not resort to such a plan even when threatened with a gigantic scheme of spoilation and sacrilege.'[34]

In spite of Napier's warning a conference of lay delegates, elected as the consultative committee suggested, met in Dublin about the middle of April.[35] The archbishops and bishops were present; some vehement speeches were made and a series of resolutions condemning the bill were passed. The conference also appointed a strong standing committee to look after the interests of the church during the parliamentary proceedings on the bill. This committee, which met frequently, suggested numerous amendments and had in London an active agent, Pilkington, a QC, who kept in close touch with the parliamentary supporters of the church. The committee also made a bold attempt to persuade the ecclesiastical commissioners to apply all the funds at their disposal 'to the use of the church without delay' and thus save as much as possible from 'confiscation'. But the paid commissioners 'held out no hope that they would consent to depart from the ordinary routine of business'.[36]

On 1 March, Gladstone in a powerful speech introduced his bill. It provided that the union between the churches of England and Ireland should be dissolved, that the Church of Ireland should cease to be an established church and that 'its property, after satisfying all just and equitable claims, should be applied for the advantage of the Irish people'. A commission, the commissioners of church temporalities, was constituted in which all the property of the church was to be vested. The existing ecclesiastical law was to be binding on members of the church, but the disestablished church was permitted to hold assemblies which could make rules for its well-being and order, and if the bishops, clergy and laity of the church appointed a representative body to hold its property, it could be incorporated by charter. One of the first duties of the church commissioners would be to arrange compensation for vested interests. A holder of an ecclesiastical benefice was to be entitled to his net income for life, so long as he continued to perform the duties attached to the benefice, and a permanent curate so long as he held his curacy was entitled to his salary. Diocesan school masters, parish clerks and sextons were to be paid so long as they performed their duties. Non-permanent curates, organists and vergers were to receive gratuities, lump sums fixed by the commissioners. A clerical annuitant could commute his life interest for a capital sum, calculated on his expectation of life and net ecclesiastical income, which would be handed over by the church commissioners to the representative church body, which would then be responsible for paying the annuitant so long as he performed his duties. Churches claimed by the representative body were to be handed over to it. Ecclesiastical residences (glebe houses and palaces) with the gardens attached were, when the representative body demanded them, to be handed over to it on the payment either of the building charges or of twelve years' annual value.[37] Private endowments granted after 1660 were to be retained by the church. It may be added that the Maynooth grant and the regium donum were also to be terminated. The trustees of Maynooth were to receive a capital sum amounting to fourteen times their annual grant, the presbyterian church was to be granted compensation on the same terms for certain annual payments it received from the state, and the presbyterian clergy were given annuities, which they might commute, based on their regium donum annual grants.

The bill was given a second reading on 23 March and, after being eleven days in committee, received its third reading on 31 May. Though during its process some powerful speeches were made and some ingenious arguments advanced, an air of inevitability hung over the debates in the commons. During the committee stage the conservatives strove to obtain better financial terms for the church – Gladstone remarked that if all their amendments had been accepted the disestablished church would have resembled Job, who after catastrophe, at the close of his life, 'had more stock and more possessions than ever'. When the bill emerged from the committee stage it was substantially unmodified and it was clear that the real struggle lay ahead when it reached the lords, where the conservatives had a large majority.

The conservative peers were influenced by conflicting motives. As hereditary legislators they instinctively sympathized with the Irish church, a venerable corporation, long part of the established order. Moreover, during the debates in the house of commons it had been driven home that disendowment was bound to weaken property rights in general. The bill, Disraeli declared, was 'a recognition of the principles of socialism'. And the 'thin end of a wedge' argument was to be employed with emphatic force by Magee in his great speech on the second reading of the bill in the lords. 'Revolutions', Magee reminded his peers, 'commence with sacrilege and go on to communism; or, to put it in the more gentle and euphemistic language of the day, revolutions begin with the church, and go on to the land.' But it might be asked, would it be wise, given the political climate of 1869, for the house of lords to reject a bill sent up by a house elected by a greatly enlarged constituency, in the first session of a new parliament? John Bright, in a published letter to his constituents, bluntly said that if the house of lords opposed the will of the nation, 'they might meet with accidents not pleasant for them to think of'. A few days before Bright wrote his letter the queen had both urged the archbishop of Canterbury to support the second reading of the bill in the lords and had written to Derby, the ex-prime minister, emphasizing that for the house of lords 'to place itself in collision with the house of commons' by throwing out the Irish church bill, would be dangerous if not disastrous.[38]

Tait had already, a month earlier, explained at a meeting of the bishops that in his opinion all that could be done in the lords was to try and amend the bill. The archbishops of Armagh and Dublin, who were at the meeting, said the Irish bishops would have to vote against the bill. 'This course', Beresford declared, 'is what the church protestants in Ireland universally propose.' And Graves of Limerick, who said that the statesmanlike course was to give the bill a second reading, was constrained to add that 'if any Irish bishop wavered he would have no opportunity of future usefulness'. Magee considered that the best course would be to give the bill a second reading and amend it, but he emphasized that the English bishops should not 'separate themselves from the Irish prelates. If the latter on behalf of the Irish church advised submission, I would submit: but if not would fight with them.'[39]

The Irish bishops were clearly afraid of losing the confidence of their laity, and Irish lay opinion was forcibly expressed at the end of May. A large and influential deputation representing the Irish church conference, the Irish presbyterians, the Ulster protestant defence association and the Irish branch of the church institute arrived in London. On 29 May the deputation met a number of peers, including the duke of Abercorn, and members of the deputation made strong speeches calling on the lords to reject the bill. Anthony Traill, a fellow of Trinity College, was cheered when he warned the peers present that if the interests of the Church of Ireland were 'postponed to those of the conservative party, that party may bid adieu to all recognition or support in Ireland'.[40] About this time Cairns, the opposition leader in the lords, an ex-lord chancellor, a fervent evangelical and a devoted son of the Church of Ireland, thought that for the lords to agree to the second reading of the bill would deprive the house of the sympathy and support of that great party in the country who were for maintaining the connection of church and state, and when on 5 June 130 conservative peers met at the duke of Marlborough's London house, he spoke in favour of rejecting the bill. Two ex-cabinet ministers, Salisbury and Carnarvon, were for giving it a second reading. It seemed to the bishop of Gloucester that Cairns spoke in the interests of his party, and Salisbury in the interests of the house of lords; Magee was for rejection and 'hang the expense'. Some 'minor Orange speakers who spoke wildly and illogically were heard with great impatience', and then Derby, the ex-prime minister, 'warmed up a slightly chilled assembly and took the line the boldest course the best course'. Finally the meeting decided in favour of rejection, the peers present being influenced, according to Magee, by two considerations – the evident determination of Gladstone to accept no amendments and the feeling that 'as they must fight on the land question, in which they have a deep personal interest, they could not and ought not to begin by yielding on the church question, in which they have less personal interest'.[41]

The debate on the second reading of the Irish church bill in the lords began on 14 June and was marked by a memorable display of Victorian parliamentary eloquence. It was also marked by great excitement – on occasions the occupants of the gallery, presumably Irishmen, in defiance of order loudly applauding speeches in defence of the Irish church. Of the Irish prelates present, Alexander of Derry made 'a decidedly effective speech but with Irish peculiarities', in which he emphasized the weakness of a church supported by voluntary contributions. Trench was despondent and out of his element (apparently he once addressed the house as 'My brethren'). According to Magee he made 'a melancholy and almost inaudible "keen" for the Irish church'. Magee himself, who thought 'this detestable bill', this 'morally iniquitous' bill should be passed, stood by his Irish friends and made a sparkling and energetic speech against it. Thirlwall, a broad churchman, and the only English bishop to support the bill, made a diffuse speech which, the bishop of Oxford remarked, 'made it easy to understand how the bishop's history of Greece was in *ten* volumes'. The speeches which seem to have counted were those of the archbishop of Canterbury, Salisbury and Carnarvon urging acceptance of the second reading. When at 3.30 on the morning of 19 June the division was taken, the second reading was carried by 174 to 146. 'I can never forget', Alexander of Derry wrote years later, 'the summer night just after the decision when I reeled out into the cool air almost hearing the crash of a great building.'[42]

But once the bill was in committee, the conservative majority asserted itself and started to try and minimize the effects of disendowment. It was decided that in calculating the net incomes of incumbents for commutation purposes the taxes paid to the ecclesiastical commissioners and salaries paid to curates (unless the curate's employment was legally obligatory) should not be deducted from the gross income. It was provided by the 'Carnarvon amendment' that the representative church body, instead of receiving a sum equal to the value of each annuity, should be paid fourteen times the aggregate incomes of all the clergy commuting. Glebe houses and small pieces of land attached to them were to be handed over to the church free of charge and the royal grants to the church made after 1560 were to be treated as private endowments. The appropriation of the surplus left in the commissioner's hands was to be settled by parliament. Finally the lords inserted in the bill a scheme which sanctioned the principle of concurrent endowment. The church commissioners were empowered to build residences for the clergy of the Church of Ireland and of the catholic and presbyterian churches.

Even before the lords began their debates on the bill, the liberal majority in the commons was beginning 'to show signs of susceptibility'.[43] And when the bill returned mutilated from the lords, the liberal party enthusiastically backed Gladstone in rejecting the principal amendments made by the lords. On two issues, however, the government made substantial concessions. Though it rejected the Carnarvon amendment, it agreed that, since clerical lives were better than the average, 7 per cent should be added to the commutation money, and it offered £500,000 in lieu of all private endowments. Addressing the opposition, Gladstone stressed that private endowments (properly so called) were probably worth only about £250,000. Addressing himself to the liberals, he pointed out that the government's offer eliminated the possibility of litigation.

By the middle of July, Gladstone was quite convinced that nothing could be said on principle for any further concession. 'The question is', he wrote, 'what we can recommend the majority to concede to the simple will of the lords rather than lose the bill.' But he was certainly not going to make concessions which would break up 'the moral union of the majority which is vital to the completion of our Irish work'. Nor was he prepared to carry the bill 'against our friends by the votes of our opponents'. Any other bill, he was sure, would give the church less generous terms on glebes and endowments. However, he thought that 'when we come to the final stage of this woeful huckstering affair we can afford £—— to be put under any head they please'.[44]

When the lords began on 20 July to reconsider the bill as returned by the commons, their temper was up. 'The debate went on,' Magee wrote,

waxing hotter and fiercer as it progressed. Argyll embittering it, and Salisbury stinging and goading the ministry, and Gladstone (who was present) to madness by his taunts, Hatherley even losing his temper and being fierce and indignant, the lords generally emulating the commons in violence and disorder, importing the element of simple insanity, which alone was wanting to the scene; and so amidst storm and fog, murky and stupefying and dirty, exit the Irish church bill.

The Irish church, Magee bitterly reflected, had been 'as I predicted from the first it would be – sacrificed to the conservative party'.[45] The lords reaffirmed several of their amendments, and it seemed as if a serious clash between the two houses was imminent. But with disestablishment and disendowment accepted in principle, the issues in dispute were relatively minor, and efforts had already been made behind the scenes to see if the differences between the two houses could be ironed out. Gladstone had seen Salisbury in June, and Salisbury had had discussions with Granville, the liberal leader in the lords, who combined firm convictions (often unpopular with his peers) with amiability and charm. Tait too was working incessantly, and after the debate on 20 July he got in touch with Granville and Gladstone, and 'urged the Irish bishops to accede to the terms', but 'found them much too afraid of their Irish friends'. On 22nd Granville and Cairns met twice, Granville between the meetings having a talk with Gladstone, and seeing Tait. Cairns, who had an able lawyer's awareness of when the time had come to compromise and who frankly admitted that by then 'money was the real object', gave up everything except three points in respect to commutation on which Granville made important concessions. The bonus was increased from 7 to 12 per cent as a payment to the church representative body for administrative expenses; the government agreed that a life interest in an ecclesiastical residence or glebe could be exempted from commutation if the occupant so desired; and the government accepted that, when an incumbent's net income was being estimated, the salary paid to a curate should not be deducted, unless the curate had been returned by the ecclesiastical commissioners as employed for five consecutive years.[46] This amendment, according to the church temporalities commissioners, had 'very singular and unexpected results'. The salaries of only 20 per cent of the curates, whose claims to compensation were accepted, were held to be deductible from the incumbent's income. Incidentally, it may be added that the church temporalities commissioners had the invidious task of deciding, in the case of curates appointed between 1 January 1869 and 1 January 1871, which appointments could be considered justified by the needs of the church, and which seemed to have been made with the object of securing compensation. They disallowed a number of claims.[47]

When the last point in their discussions was settled, Granville shook Cairns's hand, 'which was trembling with nervousness'. Later that evening the compromise was accepted by the lords in a mutually congratulatory atmosphere (only slightly marred by Salisbury's remark that Cairns 'had acted the part of a gentle Antonio to a too exacting Shylock'). The following day Gladstone, recommending the settlement to the commons, acknowledged that the opposition had fought the battle 'with the courage that becomes them as English gentlemen'.

The reactions of a keen Irish clergyman, as a settlement was emerging, were expressed by Plunket, then treasurer of St Patrick's and soon to be bishop of Tuam, in a letter to another strong upholder of the Irish church. 'You will see', Plunket wrote, 'how obstinately and mercilessly the government have refused to concede anything worth acceptance.' And though he granted that some of the conservative leaders had done their best for the church, he felt that

many who ought to be our friends are wholly indifferent – others who mean well will not apply themselves to master the really difficult intricacies of the bill – others look on the bill merely with a view to the fulfilment of their own hobbies.

Plunket concluded by declaring that

all I have seen of the way in which our church and its interests are handled by politicians who know nothing about its wants and care less about its interests makes me feel little desire to see it dragged through the mire for another six months.[48]

It might indeed be argued that when Victorian political pre-suppositions, the contemporary political climate, Irish discontent and Irish population statistics are all taken into account, disestablishment was inevitable. It may also be said that, given the inevitability of disestablishment, the financial terms granted to the disestablished church were reasonable. Other established churches have fared worse when the time came for them to be deprived of their privileged status. Nevertheless, the ablest ecclesiastical statesman in the disestablished church, writing at the close of the nineteenth century, declared that 'it may be said without exaggeration that the Irish churchmen of the last generation never quite forgave England the act of disestablishment'.[49]

III

RECONSTRUCTION

WITHIN A FEW weeks of the Irish church act receiving the royal assent, the work of reconstruction began. In August the archbishops took steps to summon their provincial synods with the object of forming a national synod. On 10 September the provincial synod of Armagh and Tuam, composed of the bishops, deans, archdeacons and proctors for the clergy, met in St Patrick's, Armagh, and accepted an invitation from the archbishop of Dublin to meet the synod of Dublin and Cashel 'in a general synod or council'. A few days later, on 14 September, the general synod met in St Patrick's cathedral, Dublin, and deliberated for three days. The bishops and the lower house agreed to record 'before God and man' 'a solemn protest against the measure whereby the imperial legislature has both deprived the Church of Ireland of the rights and confiscated the endowments which the piety of our ancestors had devoted to the service of God'. They also agreed to a preamble proposed by William Lee, the archdeacon of Dublin and archbishop King's lecturer, a redoubtable defender of the church, declaring that 'the synod is now not called upon to originate a constitution for a new communion but to repair a sudden breach in one of the most ancient churches in Christendom'. The synod approved of a scheme which provided that diocesan synods should elect representatives of the clergy who, along with the bishops and representatives of the laity, would constitute a general convention of the Church of Ireland. In the draft of this scheme, which

51

they submitted to the synod, the bishops suggested that each united diocese should be represented by a dean and an arch-deacon as well as by elected representatives. But the lower house decided that there should not be *ex officio* representatives. (Stokes, the archdeacon of Armagh, protested against this decision as 'an unnecessary departure from ancient usage which removed from the governing body of the church' 'a conservative element'.) Lee wanted the lower house to affirm that each order should sit separately in the convention and that questions of doctrine and discipline should be reserved for the bishops and clergy, while 'in all other matters the co-operation of the laity is invited'. However, it was ruled that this motion was out of order as not strictly relevant to the subject the bishops had asked the lower house to discuss. Reeves, the ecclesiastical historian, raised an interesting antiquarian issue in protesting against the admission of proctors from Emly, contending that the dioceses of Cashel and Emly were fused.[1]

At the beginning of August a meeting of delegates to the national church conference, including twenty-one noblemen and MPs, asked the archbishops to re-convene the conference. The archbishops declined to do so on the ground that the conference had been assembled for a specific purpose, to oppose the Irish church bill. A few weeks later at the end of August a large meeting of influential laymen decided that there should be a lay conference to determine how the representatives of the laity in church assemblies should, in the future, be chosen. Having turned down the suggestion that the dukes of Abercorn and Leinster should summon such a conference, the meeting requested the archbishop to do so.[2] The archbishops issued their summons, and parish representatives chose delegates to a lay conference which on 12 October met in Dublin at the Moles-worth Hall. On assembling, the delegates discovered that the archbishops were awaiting them at the Antient Concert Rooms to which the assembly at once adjourned. The confer-ence decided that when the bishops and representatives of the clergy and laity met, each order should have the right to call for a vote by orders (it being left uncertain whether the bishops should vote separately or be included in the clerical order). Bence Jones, a county Cork landlord, who could express himself vigorously, wrote, 'I believe a lot of the northerners were ready to vote to abolish bishops bodily . . . one fellow was heard to say "Vote by orders. I won't vote by the orders of any man".[3] However the duke of Abercorn, a great Ulster landowner, urging the conference to agree to voting by orders, tactfully argued that a vote by orders would favour the laity, since the clergy would probably prove to be the more steady attenders. It was also decided that in diocesan synods and the national synod the lay representation should be to the clerical in the ratio of two to one. Two arguments were advanced in favour of this. It was asserted that the clergy would attend better, and it was also pointed out that if the lay representation was left equal to the clerical, then, assuming the assemblies were not permitted to be too large, the middle-class layman would find himself excluded from the councils of his church. There was an animated debate on the geographical distribution of representation, some northern delegates being anxious that numbers should receive due weight. In the end a compromise which took into account population and the parochial system (and which, Bence Jones complained 'put us at the mercy of the north') was arrived at. The question of whether women should be permitted to be parochial electors was raised, but was summarily disposed of.[4]

In February 1870 the bishops and the representatives of the clergy and laity met to form a general convention of the Church of Ireland. This body, which gathered in the Antient Concert Rooms in Great Brunswick Street, held two sessions, one of forty-one days' duration at the beginning of the year, the other, a comparatively short one, of sixteen days near its close. During these sessions the convention accomplished a tremendous amount of urgent, complex and detailed work, approving a constitution for the church, setting up a system of ecclesiastical courts and arranging for the formation of a representative body to hold and manage the church's property.[5]

The outlines of a constitution had emerged during the lay and clerical meetings in September and October. Moreover, when framing a constitution, the Church of Ireland started with the advantage that the episcopal churches of the USA, Canada and New Zealand had already faced this problem. Their constitutions were available to Irish churchmen in a convenient form, having been printed in a single volume published in 1868 by William Sherlock, a county Meath clergyman. Incidentally, when providing constitutional documentation, Sherlock drew Irish churchmen's attention to the fact that in the American church, power in respect to finance and patronage had been granted to parishes to an extent which was detrimental to the general interests of the church.[6]

The constitution, sanctioned by the general convention, set up and made rules for a hierarchy of governing bodies, the parochial select vestry, diocesan synods and the general synod. The select vestry, elected by the registered vestrymen (the suggestion that women might be members of vestries was rejected by 158 votes to 108), controlled the parochial funds. In each diocese there was to be a diocesan synod, any such synod being empowered to unite with any other synod in the united dioceses. The diocesan synod, which was to be responsible for the administration of the temporalities of the church in the diocese, was composed of the bishop, the beneficed and licensed clergy of the diocese and lay representatives chosen by the parishes, it being provided that the ratio of lay to clerical representation should be as two to one. The synod was to elect a diocesan council and to select a clergyman and two laymen who were, with the bishop, to form the diocesan committee of patronage. When a cure in the diocese became vacant, this committee, together with three nominators selected by the parish, was responsible for filling the vacancy. When a diocese was vacant the diocesan synod – or the synods of a united diocese meeting together – elected the bishop. If no person secured the requisite majority of votes, then the vacancy would be filled by the episcopal bench. The question of filling a vacancy in the see of Armagh presented a problem, since the archbishop of Armagh was not only a diocesan bishop but the primate. At first it was decided that, on a vacancy in Armagh, the diocese should make a list comprising the names of four members of the bench of bishops and the bench should select the archbishop from this list. Second thoughts, however, prevailed. It was finally decided that, in a vacancy in the see of Armagh, the diocesan synod should elect an *ad interim* bishop who should join with the other members of the bench in electing the new primate from amongst the members of the bench. If the *ad interim* bishop was not elected to Armagh, he would become the bishop of the diocese vacated by the new primate.

This method of episcopal selection lasted for almost sixty years. But in 1939 an experimental era set in. On the grounds that 'it was expedient that every diocese should participate in the selection of a bishop for the church', it was then enacted that there should be constituted a board of selectors, clerical and lay in equal numbers, drawn from all the dioceses. When a diocese was vacant, this board formed a select list of names from which the diocesan synod was to elect. When Armagh fell vacant, the bishops, together with a clerical representative from Armagh, who would not be eligible for election to the archbishopric, would select an archbishop for Armagh. At the end of six years this system was set aside, it being enacted in 1945 that, when an episcopal vacancy occurred, the standing committee of the general synod was to prepare a select list of names which were to be added to those on a list which would be prepared by the synod of the vacant diocese. From this final list the synod would elect. This system lasted for fourteen years and then in 1959 a third method was adopted. Since 'it was expedient that provision should be made for more general representation of the members of the Church of Ireland in the election of bishops of the church', an electoral college was constituted. It was composed of the archbishop of the province (or of the bishop next in precedence), of three bishops, and of lay and clerical representatives from each diocese. At an election the representation of the vacant diocese was to be somewhat increased. If Armagh was vacant the bishops were to elect an archbishop from their own body.

The diocesan synods elected the members of the house of representatives. The general synod was composed of two houses, the house of bishops and the house of representatives, the houses voting and sitting together, except when the bishops expressed a desire to consider separately a matter in debate. In each diocese there was to be a diocesan court composed of the bishop and his chancellor, together with a clergyman and a layman elected by the diocesan synod to whom questions of fact would be referred. From the diocesan courts there was an appeal to the court of the general synod, composed of an archbishop and three laymen taken from a list drawn up by the general synod, the list being composed of persons who had been judges in a superior court or (after 1893) QCs who had acted as diocesan chancellors for at least five years.

The constitutional issue which aroused the most intense feeling was the position to be assigned to the bishops in the councils of the church. The draft constitution had proposed that a question should only be deemed to be carried in the general synod if assented to by a majority of each house. In place of this provision, a leading low churchman proposed that if a measure which had been rejected by the bishops should, on being reintroduced, be carried by two-thirds of both the clerical and lay order, then it would become law. The duke of Abercorn suggested a compromise which was accepted by an overwhelming majority. It provided that if a question, affirmed by the house of representatives and rejected by a majority of the bishops, was in the following session reaffirmed by a two-thirds majority of the house of representatives, voting as a body or by orders, then it would be deemed to be carried, 'unless it be negatived by not less than two-thirds of the entire existing order of bishops, the said two-thirds being present and voting', and giving their reasons in writing.

The constitution has proved basically sound, having endured for a century. Its elaborate system of representative bodies and committees bound churchmen together, gave the laity considerable weight in the councils of the church and made considerable demands on their time and energy. In fact it might be said that the constitution presumed a leisured laity. This existed in the post-disestablishment age, many protestant gentlemen who felt that they were being pushed out of local public life finding in the councils of their church an outlet for their political energies and aptitudes. Also, as might have been expected, in the years following disestablishment a number of the clergy found that working in a church in which so much power was now possessed by the laity was somewhat irksome. This is clearly revealed by the answers to a questionnaire on the recruitment of the clergy circulated to incumbents in 1878.[7] The replies to the question 'what obstacles prevented suitable candidates for orders coming forward?' may not furnish a reliable guide to the attitudes of youth in the 1870s, but they undoubtedly reflect the feelings of those parochial clergymen who replied. Many of them strongly resented the extent to which the laity were interfering in ecclesiastical affairs. A county Donegal incumbent complained that the laity had become so exacting that they expected 'more than mortal man can do'. And a Limerick clergyman summed up his feelings in the phrase, 'more work and less talk from the laity'. The new patronage system especially aroused clerical resentment and criticism. It was humiliating, it was said, for educated men to have to depend on the judgment of ignorant and intolerant parochial nominators, 'better fitted to be judges of a *horse*, a *dog* or even a *pig*'. What impressed the nominators, it was declared, was a showy sermon, and if a young man displayed intellectual originality it was assumed he was a ritualist. It may be added that it was not only the parochial clergy who were critical of the patronage system. Salmon felt that the new system 'in striving to avoid the faults of the old . . . has gone too far in the opposite direction'. Before disestablishment, patrons had, in Salmon's opinion, paid considerable attention to 'the claims of the clergyman and awarded a deserving man without thinking much of the needs of the church'. The parochial nominators on the other hand tended to think only of the future needs of their parish. Reichel, who had strongly supported the adoption of the system, later thought that the diocese should have more weight and the parishioners less, when an incumbent was being appointed.[8]

When the general synod met for the first time in 1871, a new code of canons was approved. Apparently about 350 of the clergy exercised their right under the Irish church act to dissent from the new canons and remain bound by the Irish canon law as it existed at the time of disestablishment, the redoubtable Lee, characteristically, protesting against 'the narrow and intolerant spirit which pervades this wearisome catalogue of minute and unprofitable negatives'.[9] The revision of the prayer book was also taken in hand. It was not an opportune season for liturgical revision. Anglican thought was being influenced by strong and conflicting currents. Broad churchmen were demanding that contemporary scientific discovery and the results of modern biblical criticism should be taken into account. High churchmen, inspired by the tractarian revival, were emphasizing the catholic elements in the church's tradition and reviving or introducing ceremonial usages which they believed symbolized doctrinal truth and added to the beauty and dignity of public worship. Evangelicals, who, if they had never been predominant in the church, had for long seen themselves as the most active, vivifying and popular force in anglicanism, were dismayed by these developments, which they were convinced, would undermine true religious faith. Many of the new ideas and theories in scientific thought were profoundly shaking. But it was changes or threatened changes in public worship which aroused widespread excitement and anger. Plain men were shocked by departures from the familiar pattern of English public worship, and exasperated to discover that rules, the conventional interpretation of which had long been taken for granted, were ambiguous and difficult to enforce. High church-men who introduced new practices asserted that the 'ornaments rubric', far from being a restraint on their actions, positively enjoined the innovations which were being attacked, and they boldly challenged the jurisdiction of courts which they contended rested on Erastian error.

Members of the Irish bench were quick to censure *Essays and Reviews*. But it was the growth of ritualism which aroused wide-spread alarm amongst Irish churchmen. Salmon, shortly after he became regius professor of divinity, in an essay dealing with the ritualists said that 'their whole proceedings' were 'character-ized by wilfulness, private judgment and contempt of lawful authority'.[10] 'What mean these miserable men in England', asked John Gregg of Cork, 'in disturbing the church and troubling the minds of the people with their frippery in doctrine and trumpery in dress?'[11] Admittedly, ritualism was a cross-channel phenomenon. In Ireland the influence of evangelicalism and surrounding strength of Roman catholicism made church-men instinctively distrustful of ceremonial change. Even high churchmen, such as Maturin, departed only cautiously from the customary pattern. An austere dignity of worship reflected their churchmanship and had strong roots in the Anglo-Irish respect for emotional control and a self-respecting restraint when facing the crises of life. But the Church of Ireland did not remain completely immune from the mid-century liturgical movement. About the time of disestablishment, proceedings in three Dublin churches, St Bride's, St Bartholomew's and All

Saints', aroused considerable excitement. Carroll of St Bride's, an irrepressible controversialist, in 1866 introduced a choral service. Grave disorders broke out on Sunday 8 April. Members of the congregation, loudly repeating the responses while the choir was singing the service, produced 'a perfect Babel of tongues'. During the recital of the creed for which Carroll turned east, hissing began and during the sermon there were cries of 'No popery' and 'Go to Rome'. Finally Carroll, 'pale and collected', withdrew and the police cleared the church. A few days later the churchwardens announced that Mr Carroll, who was unwell, had agreed to discontinue the practices which had caused the disorder.[12] A year earlier the foundation stone of St Bartholomew's was laid. Built in a new prosperous middle-class area, St Bartholomew's was, in the words of the first incumbent of the parish, Arthur Dawson, a church where the pews were free and 'the old fashioned principles of the prayer book, at present little valued in Ireland', were preached. Shortly after it was opened, zealous protestants were disturbed to observe 'a gaudily coloured cloth in front of, and flowers on the communion table, and a ledge at the back of the table, "a super-altar".'[13]

The incumbent of Grangegorman, William Maturin, son of the novelist and father of Basil Maturin, the Roman catholic preacher and author, was regarded by some as the greatest preacher in the Church of Ireland. A stern tractarian, with strong convictions which he set out in the simplest and clearest words, he was not a ritualist. But, in the words of a young sympathizer, 'the moderate ecclesiastical decencies of his church ... seemed sheer Romanism' to many Dublin protestants and caused disturbances. One of Maturin's congregation was D'Arcy, a country gentleman (uncle of a future primate), who took a house in the parish to qualify as a member of the vestry. 'His stalwart form, on more than one occasion, held the door against intruders' bent on making known their dissent from the rector's teaching, and on occasion Mahaffy heard Maturin himself 'crush by his fiery words a mob of young men who came to disturb his services on protestant principles and drive them cowed and slinking from his church'. In 1872 Maturin was charged in the archbishop of Dublin's court with saying public prayer with his back to the congregation, with intoning services, with bowing to the Lord's table and with having 'an embroidered lace and striped coloured cloth on the table'. Maturin lodged a protest, in which he declared that the court was not one 'existing by the law of the church or constituted by lawful authority'. But, it having been pointed out that the Church of Ireland was now a voluntary society the rules of which were binding on its members, Maturin was tried and admonished for turning his back on the people during public prayers.[14]

It was, however, the action of a curate attached to the Dublin church of St Stephen's, the ritual in which aroused no comment, which provoked the most widespread and vehement outburst of protestant feeling. He gave a maidservant, being prepared for confirmation, a small manual, *Short prayers for those who have but little time to pray*. Her master, a strong low churchman, wrote to the archbishop to know if he approved of its contents. Trench refused to censure the manual and the question was discussed at numerous vestry meetings – the meeting at St Peter's being especially lively because the rector, archdeacon Lee, a strong high churchman, refused to allow the question to be discussed and, 'having mounted a chair', adjourned the meeting. Two addresses, each signed by about eighty clergy in the diocese, were presented to the archbishop. The first condemned the manual, the second – apparently prepared by Dickinson, dean of the chapel royal, a witty broad churchman – declared that the signatories could not see why the archbishop 'should be urged to pass beyond the bounds of his lawful authority and curtail that liberty of judgment and action which is enjoyed by the lay as well as the clerical members of our church'.[15]

To many Irish churchmen it seemed as if ritualism might spread fast if counter-measures were not taken promptly. Towards the middle of October 1870 William Brooke, a master in chancery, a devout supporter of the church and a fervent evangelical, presented to the general convention a widely signed memorial requesting 'the adoption of all such precautions as may be necessary to preserve our church from the encroachment of modern ritualism'. The convention responded by appointing a committee to enquire into what measures should be taken 'to check the spread of doctrines and practices opposed to the principles of our reformed church', without making 'any alterations in the liturgy and formularies of the church as would imply a change in her doctrines'. The committee, 'Master Brooke's committee', considering that its duty was to check 'modern ritualism' by striking at its basis, 'the assumption to the priesthood of powers which do not belong to that office', suggested a number of changes in the communion and ordination services and in the office for the visitation of the sick. But when the work of the committee was discussed in the general synod of 1871, a substantial section of the synod obviously felt that the committee had gone to work in an over-ruthless and partisan fashion. Salmon, urging that 'the time had arrived for a revision of the formularies in a cautious and reverent spirit', secured the election of a new large and somewhat broader committee to co-operate with the bishops in the work of revising the liturgy. Shortly afterwards Salmon published a simple, direct, powerful pamphlet in which he urged that 'Christ's church on earth should not be narrower than his church in Heaven'. He also produced a very practical argument against extreme revisionism. If the high churchmen were driven out of the church, they would form congregations in Ireland in communion with the Church of England. These congregations would have numerous adherents and the Church of Ireland might find itself reduced to being 'a local sect'.[16]

The revision committee, after holding a number of meetings, reported to the general synod in 1872. During the sessions of 1872–4 its recommendations were discussed; the results of the discussions were incorporated in bills passed in the session of 1875 and a preface to the prayer book was sanctioned in 1877. In addition, in 1873 a new lectionary was approved and a hymnal based on the report of the committee on church hymnology was 'permitted for use in the public worship of the Church of Ireland'. The committee took as the basis of its report a church hymnal published for use in Ireland by the SPCK in 1864, adding and removing a number of hymns. Two authors who were well represented were members of the Church of Ireland, Sir Edward Denny, sometime MP for Tralee, who became a leader of the Plymouth Brethren, and Cecil Frances Alexander, whose husband became bishop of Derry in 1867. Mrs Alexander's hymns, with their controlled intensity of feeling and sensitive simplicity of diction, are among the finest expressions of the piety of the age.

The revision discussions and debates were lengthy and some-times passionate. Men were deeply conscious that they were dealing with the expression of saving truths and often spoke with profound feeling. Many of those who took part in the pro-ceedings, Alexander, Trench, Fitzgerald, Lloyd (the provost of Trinity), Plunket, Reichel, Reeves, Salmon, Travers Smith, possessed erudition, intellectual force and eloquence. Reichel, probably the most learned of those who favoured fairly thorough-going revision, had been born a moravian and had been educated for some years in Germany before entering Trinity. A sometime professor of Latin in Queen's College, Belfast, and later bishop of Meath, he was a broad churchman of evangeli-cal sympathies. A man of wide and solid learning he could express himself forcibly – a strong anti-revisionist remarked, 'his bitter tongue did not belie the expression of his face' (which, if a photograph may be relied on, suggests a man of impatient temper who would not suffer fools willingly).[17] Another leading revisionist was Plunket, later archbishop of Dublin, an evan-gelical with a broad church bias. An ecclesiastical statesman, the grandson of a great lord chancellor, Plunket was prepared to make concessions for the sake of unity. But to some he seemed ready to go too far. It was said that during the revision dis-cussions Alexander of Derry was seen 'coming out of the committee room with an expression of disgust on his face'. Someone asked him what was going on inside. He replied, 'Oh nothing. Nothing. Only the usual thing. Plunket is preparing an amendment to the Lord's Prayer.'[18]

A powerful group of laymen, amongst whom Napier, Bloomfield, General Dunne, Colonel Ffolliott, Saunderson, Kavanagh, and Lord James Butler were prominent, strongly favoured revision on protestant lines and mustered a large amount of support, especially among the lay representatives. Lord James Butler, an uncle of the marquess of Ormonde, a tall handsome bearded and ebullient retired army officer, was a fervent and fluent low churchman, very critical of the episcopal bench. Kavanagh, born without limbs, was a public-spirited country gentleman, an improving landlord and an active MP. Saunderson, later an exuberant leader of the Irish unionists in the

fight against home rule, was renowned for his skill as a yachts-
man, his quick humorous retorts and his readiness to engage in a
political shindy. A strong evangelical, on Sundays he preached
simple, direct sermons in a church on his estate. Napier, an
ex-lord chancellor and a member of the 1867 royal commission
on ritual, was a very able lawyer whose devotion to the church
had earned him the nickname 'Holy Joe'. The two outstanding
conservative leaders were the archbishop of Armagh and the
bishop of Derry. Trench, highly sensitive and somewhat
pessimistic, was devoted to the prayer book. He was afraid that
ruthless revision might end in the Church of Ireland sanctioning
heresy and separating itself from the Church of England and
he clearly found the tone of much of the discussion very
distasteful. On one occasion his control snapped and he
referred in the general synod to their 'miserable debates' –
producing a scene which ended in Trench's explaining that by
'miserable' he meant 'unhappy'.[19] Alexander of Derry was
more resilient. A spirited debater, he wrote years afterwards,
'I nailed my colours to the mast – rightly in many instances I
still think – but with unnecessary defiance.'[20] One of the most
outspoken of the high church clergy was Richard Travers
Smith, curate of St Bartholomew's, who, preaching at Trench's
visitation of 1872, expressed the fear that the Church of Ireland
might become 'a church of half assertions and diluted doctrines'.
Another strong conservative was Reeves, the great ecclesiastical
historian. He seldom spoke, but in the words of his biographer he
'always voted with the minority who protested against every
change in doctrine and practice'.

The major questions round which debate surged were the
Athanasian creed, the communion office, the baptismal
service and the ordinal. There had developed in England a
movement to remove the creed from the liturgy, or to omit the
'damnatory clauses' or at least to insert a rubric explaining (or
some would say explaining away) their significance. Many Irish
laymen disliked reciting these clauses and the revision committee suggested their omission. Trench opposed this suggestion
– 'the creed', he declared, 'lopped at the beginning, lopped at
the end, lopped in the middle', reminded him of 'unhappy
victims of oriental cruelty'.[21] But he was willing to agree to a
rubric stating that the 'so-called condemnatory clauses' only

applied to those who, possessing the knowledge, denied the substance of the Christian faith. After much discussion it was finally decided to leave the creed in the prayer book but to omit the rubric enjoining its use. The form of absolution in the office for the visitation of the sick was replaced by that used in the communion office; and a series of attempts was made to amend the 'black rubric' (which excluded the adoration of the elements) by adding a sentence strengthening its import. The more eager revisionists wanted to remove from the baptismal service the phrases suggesting regeneration, and in the ordination service they wanted the words 'Receive the Holy Ghost . . . whose sins thou dost remit . . .' altered. They were defeated on both issues, it being argued that if the ordinal was changed, Irish clergy ordained according to the new form might not be considered by the Church of England to be in holy orders. Napier defended the existing form of ordination in an eloquent speech. He admitted that 'if they went up north and gave the sturdy people there to understand that it [the ordinal] contained any of the sentiments or flavoured aught of popery the agitation and outcry would continue'. So he called on the synod 'to tell the country emphatically' that the ordinal was the production of the reformers.[22]

A number of new prayers and thanksgivings were placed in the new prayer book and more flexibility was permitted in the use of the liturgy. One aim of the rubrics and the canons relating to public worship was to prevent the adoption of practices favoured by ritualists in England. In fact a resolute effort was made to stereotype by law in the Church of Ireland the forms of worship customary in contemporary anglicanism. It may be added that the regulations relating to ritual and ornaments were enacted with relatively little discussion. Indeed, canon thirty-six, which forbade the placing of a cross on the communion table, a canon which later was the subject of heated controversy, was seemingly agreed to without debate in a thin house.[23]

The preface to the new prayer book, which was largely devoted to explaining that the controversial phrases in the liturgy which remained unchanged could be interpreted in a way acceptable to low churchmen, was strongly attacked by the bishop of Derry, who declared that its tendency 'taken as a whole was in a sort of semi-sceptical direction to make men doubtful ... minimizing and paring away their belief', and by the archbishop of Dublin, who complained that it was 'a seed plot full of the possibilities of dissention', 'wholly and absolutely unnecessary'.[24] (Trench's friend Pusey, on seeing a draft of the preface, had remarked that its 'Jesuitry far outdoes that of Rome'.) When the preface was finally placed before the synod for approval, the bishops, voting as a separate body, agreed to its enactment by only five votes to four (the minority including the two archbishops and two future primates, Alexander and Knox). It may be added that the composers of the preface tried to answer all the critics of the revised book (and the critics of the preface) in advance by asking their readers 'to consider that men's judgments of perfection are very various, and what is imperfect with peace is often better than what is otherwise more excellent without it'.

It is remarkable, after the long-drawn-out controversies and excitement of the revision era, how few significant changes were made in the prayer book. One important constitutional provision which reflected the cautious conservatism of those classes, country gentlemen, lawyers and clergy, which predominated in the councils of the disestablished church, strongly favoured that 'great but to a great extent noiseless body who were opposed to change, who liked things as they were and who did not like to be coerced by majorities of more active people'.[25] It had been provided in the constitution approved by the convention of 1870 in a clause enacted, apparently with scarcely any discussion, that no bill for the purpose of making any alteration in the articles, doctrine, rubrics or rites of the church should be introduced except on a resolution, passed in full synod, by a two-thirds majority of each order. This meant that a minority of either of the orders, if it comprised at least a third, could block attempts at liturgical change. It would also probably be true to say that some synodsmen who displayed liturgical radicalism by voting for changes, nevertheless, once the excitement was over, were well content to hear the familiar phrases.

During its first session the general convention prepared a draft charter for the representative body which was to hold the church's property and manage its finances. It was decided that this body should be composed of the archbishops and bishops, and of a clerical and lay representative from each of the united dioceses. In addition there were to be co-opted members equal in number to the number of united dioceses. Before the middle of March the elected members had been chosen and the co-opted members selected. And by April the representative church body was hard at work (it was called at first the representative body of the church, but in the royal charter granted in October 1870 it was styled the representative church body). It had an immense amount to accomplish, much of which had to be done quickly. As it was pointed out later, unlike most great financial corporations which grow from small beginnings, the representative church body found itself from the outset in control of a large capital and faced with heavy responsibilities.

If the administrative continuity and cohesion of the church was to be maintained and its organization adapted to meet future needs, it was essential that the clergy should commute, and one of the first steps taken by the representative body was to draw up a code of rules relating to commuting and compounding and to appoint a commutation committee which during the two years 1871 and 1872 sat 211 times, its sittings being frequently 'long and laborious, as a single case of commutation sometimes involved the examination of very complicated proposals and a long correspondence'.[26] Commutation meant that men brought up in the security of the establishment had to choose quickly between accepting an annuity guaranteed by the state or depending for an income on the financial acumen of a new and untried body, embarking perforce on a large-scale insurance scheme. Many might well have hesitated. But the great majority of the clergy were loyal to their church.[27] By the close of 1875, 2,059 had commuted, the non-commutators amounting to only 101.[28] In every diocese well over three-quarters of the clergy had commuted so that the bonus was secured on all the commutation money, and the representative church body received from the church temporalities commissioners £7,580,000. Theoretically this capital would have been exhausted when all the annuities had been paid. In fact by 1886 it was clear to the representative body that after all claims on the commutation fund had been made it would have about £3,000,000 in hand. There were at least two reasons for this. The representative church body pursued an investment policy which secured a higher rate of interest on their capital than had been allowed for when the value of the annuities were being calculated. Second, the representative church body was willing to enter into arrangements with clergymen who wished to 'compound'. A compounder received part of the capital value of his annuity down, the representative church body retaining the remaining part, and was released from the obligation to continue serving in the Church of Ireland. Of those who had commuted by the close of 1874–5, 750 had also compounded. Years later Stephen Gwynn recalled an exciting episode of this era. At the very time when Alexander of Derry's life interest was being negotiated, the Rev. John Gwynn, 'financier in chief to the diocese', was dismayed to see the bishop, weighing eighteen stone, being sculled in a currach by a daring curate through the rocks and currents of Mulroy Bay, 'a hundred thousand pounds of ecclesiastical capital divided from submersion by a piece of tarred calico'.[29]

The representative church body from the outset, of course, realized that the funds handed over to it at disestablishment would be insufficient to meet the church's long-term needs. It had the sound Victorian instinct not to eat into capital if it could be avoided, and it was anxious 'to save the church from the ordinary evils of the voluntary system', and 'to guard it against the dangers inherent in a purely congregational system'. Therefore it set to work with energy, urgency and imagination to build up a sustentation fund. A strongly worded appeal was issued, accompanied by practical suggestions for fund raising. Each diocesan synod was to be responsible for the drive in its own area. Adherents of the church were to be canvassed, and it was suggested that landowners and farmers should give sixpence in the pound on their valuation and that wage-earners should give a week's wages.[30] The result was certainly impressive. In the early 1880s it was estimated that in the eleven years following disestablishment well over £2,000,000 had been contributed, and by 1906 the total contribution had swollen to over £6,500,000. By a crude but effective financial test Irish episcopalians had proved their loyalty to their church.

The representative church body took early steps to decentralize to some extent the financial administration of the Church of

Ireland. Each diocese was instructed to frame a financial 'scheme' for meeting its ecclesiastical requirements. The diocese was credited by the representative church body with the profits of commutation and compounding and with subscriptions to the sustentation fund earmarked for its use. It was expected to settle parochial boundaries, decide how many clergy it could support and the parochial assessments to the stipend fund. The representative church body acted as a banker for the dioceses, receiving the assessment money, paying stipends and managing the diocesan capital. In addition the representative body was responsible for a multiplicity of trust funds, 'specific trusts' in 1914 requiring 4,000 separate accounts. Moreover, about 1,630 churches and nearly 900 glebes were vested in it, and it bought back from the church temporalities commissioners 900 ecclesiastical residences, including twelve episcopal palaces. From the beginning the representative church body showed remarkable frankness, publishing yearly statements which soon swelled into a fat annual volume with pages of detailed accounts. It could be firm in dealing with its clients. Shortly after it was established, it sent back to a number of dioceses their claims for churches and glebes which were to be transmitted to the church temporalities commission because they were set out badly. And, finding that many of the glebe houses it took over were in a very dilapidated condition, the representative body promptly drafted stringent rules – probably not always palatable to the occupants – for inspection and repair.[31]

In one respect the Church of Ireland was remarkably fortunate. Disestablishment came at a time when the Irish landlords were comparatively prosperous and apparently secure, and during the era of reconstruction they subscribed generously to the funds of their church. Towards the close of the 1870s, however, the great agricultural depression started; and 1879 marked the beginning of prolonged and widespread agrarian unrest in Ireland. By the middle 1880s it had come to be generally accepted that the Irish question could best be solved by removing the landlord from the agrarian system and turning the tenants into owner-occupiers. 'Things have come to such a pass', an Irish landowner wrote in 1885, 'that the landlords must be got rid of; so long as they are there to be plundered and worried there will be no peace in the country.'[32] The land purchase acts offered terms which on the whole were not unattractive – estates were often burdened with heavy charges, landlords in the south and west were usually both politically and theologically out of sympathy with their tenants, and the collection of rents could be a contentious operation. Moreover, the democratization of Irish local government in 1898 deprived the Irish landed class of much of their prestige and power, and home rule was always on the horizon. So the steady sale of estates began. Many landed families left, others, even though they kept their house and demesne, were bound in time to go. This process not only involved the breaking up of many large protestant households, but meant in many parishes the disappearance of the leading members of the Church of Ireland community and the loss of the principal subscribers to parish funds.

In its report for 1880 the representative body noted that the classes which paid a large part of the diocesan assessment for stipends had 'suffered severely from the recent commercial and agricultural depression', and in 1887 it observed that a large sum representing unpaid interest on mortgage loans was outstanding – an indication that many Irish landlords were in difficulties. It is true that the representative body recovered a considerable proportion of the arrears on interest which piled up during the disturbed years when estates were sold and their encumbrances paid off. With land purchase the amount lent on mortgage declined and by 1914 the representative body's investments in land mortgages amounted to only about £1,000,000, compared to about £3,400,000 in 1885. This presented the problem of finding suitable alternative outlets for investment. Even in the early 1880s the representative body had been impressed by the high price of debentures and preference shares, and in 1906 it declared that the shift from mortgages to other investments involved a fall in the rate of interest received from $4\frac{1}{2}$ to $3\frac{1}{2}$ per cent.

Understandably, then, from the early 1890s great efforts were being made to bring home to all members of the Church of Ireland – and more especially to the farming community – their financial responsibilities to their church. Also at the beginning of the twentieth century a great effort was made to increase the capital controlled by the representative church body. In 1904 a drive was begun to raise an auxiliary fund, the interest on which would help to meet the loss consequent on the shift from mortgage investment, and by 1913 this fund amounted to £260,000. The careful husbanding of resources and the generosity of members of the church is shown by the way in which the representative church body's capital grew from £7,000,000 in 1881 to £9,470,000 in 1913. By the latter year the pattern of investment was assuming the shape it retained until the later 1940s. A very small amount of mortgages, a very substantial amount (about 50 per cent of the total capital) in government securities (home, colonial and foreign), and the remainder in corporation stocks, and railways and public utilities (preference and debenture shares). In managing this capital, the representative body had to sustain some severe shocks. In 1919 it noted that the interest on nearly £100,000 invested in Russian bonds 'had not been received', and in 1933 that the church's 'income had suffered owing in a large measure to the loss on railway preference securities'. However, the representative body was careful to build up reserves to meet the investment losses, it was aided between 1914 and the early 1930s by relatively high interest rates, and in 1939 its capital assets stood at £11,180,000.

By energetic, well planned activity the Church of Ireland after disestablishment obtained the financial resources it required, activity which provided a striking illustration of the new importance of laymen in the life of the church. From 1871 the Church of Ireland was a self-governing body; with self-government came a great increase in the power of the laity and power was accompanied by a strong sense of responsibility. Nearly forty years after the Irish church act was passed, Traill, the provost of Trinity, a robust layman with plenty of practical acumen who played a very active part in the councils of the church, wrote

that while much worldly or financial injustice was done to the members of the church by that act, much spiritual advantage has accrued to them from their being as it were forced to realise what are the duties of the church and its members.[33]

IV

THE FIRST FORTY YEARS OF
DISESTABLISHMENT

~~~~~~

ONCE THE DEBATES on reconstruction and revision were
ended, the Church of Ireland entered on a long period of
internal peace and institutional stability – an era which lasted
certainly until 1914 and indeed in many respects endured until
1939. It is, of course, tempting to emphasize the contrast between
the placidity of ecclesiastical history and the stress and storm of
secular politics. Irish history in the last quarter of the nineteenth and the first quarter of the twentieth centuries was
marked by important and dramatic events: the land war, land
purchase and the establishment of a peasant proprietorship, the
Gaelic revival, the literary revival, the home rule struggle, the
1916 rebellion, the efforts to assert Irish independence between
1919 and 1921, the civil war, the emergence of the Irish Free
State and Northern Ireland. Nevertheless it might be argued
that, in spite of the political excitement and intellectual ferment
of the time, Ireland as a whole was a community which changed
very slowly. During the Irish railway age the industrial pattern
did not alter dramatically and the countryside and the medium-
sized and small country towns maintained their nineteenth-
century tempo and way of life until well into the twentieth
century. Of course landlordism vanished after some years of
serious agrarian strife, marked by refusals to pay rent, evictions,
boycotting and sporadic outrage. But very often a landlord,

71

when selling his estate, retained possession of his house and the demesne. The 1912 edition of Burke's *Landed gentry* – the golden book of the Irish landed world – records nearly all the families it lists as residing in their ancestral seats, and the disappearance of the landed gentry from wide stretches of the Irish countryside was the result of a long process of erosion. There was, of course, from the middle 1880s the disturbing possibility that the nationalists might succeed in winning home rule for Ireland. To most Irish protestants home rule was detestable and alarming, but the defeat of two home rule bills, a long period of unionist predominance in British politics and the overwhelming unionist majority in the house of lords all contributed to keep the prospect of home rule at a distance, and in 1914 the political framework was fundamentally the same as in 1870.

The slow rate of change within the Church of Ireland is well illustrated by the episcopal bench. Alexander, the last of the pre-disestablishment bishops, did not retire until 1911 and nine of his fellow diocesans at the time of his retirement had been ordained before disestablishment. And as late as 1923 there was on the bench a bishop who had worked for some years as a clergyman in the established church. At the time of disestablishment the Church of Ireland had two archbishops and ten bishops but in 1886, with Clogher being again separated from Armagh, the membership of the bench was raised to thirteen. Between 1872 and 1914 twenty-nine new bishops were elected. Of the twenty-nine new bishops, twenty-eight had had parochial experience as incumbents. The exception was Bernard, who was a fellow of Trinity before he went to the deanery of St Patrick's, from whence he was promoted to the bishopric of Ossory – though it might be said that Plunket, who became bishop of Meath in 1876, was a parochial clergyman only for a short time in special circumstances. For eight years he was incumbent of Kilmoylin in the diocese of Tuam, a living with four Church of Ireland parishioners. In fact Plunket was busily employed acting as secretary to his uncle, the bishop. A number of the bishops elected in the forty years following disestablishment were men of considerable intellectual distinction. Reichel, elected bishop of Meath in 1885, seemed to the young Henley Henson, 'a formidable critic of unsound assumptions, unwarranted assertions, faulty reasoning and the taking bombast of mere rhetoric'.[1] Chadwick of Derry was a forcible preacher prepared to tackle difficult problems; Reeves of Down was a learned ecclesiastical historian; D'Arcy, elected to Down in 1911 when working as a parochial clergyman, had built up a reputation as an academic philosopher which led to his becoming a fellow of the British Academy; Berry of Killaloe wrote on the relationship of Christianity and other faiths. There were, too, on the bench a number of men of strong personality – O'Hara of Cashel (the first dean of Belfast), Elliott of Kilmore, who to an extraordinary degree fused fiery enthusiasm for his church with a shrewd grasp of practical detail, and Stack of Clogher, who, as archbishop Benson wrote in 1896, was 'a really marvellous man – aged 72, most upright, clear-eyed, quick, light-stepping man equal to any fatigue – was brought up upon Lough Erne, knows every gentleman, farmer and labourer in his diocese and every haunt of pike and trout in the whole lough – every rock and island – breeds and keeps the best horses, and is a great gardener and withal a faithful pastor'.[2] It may be added that Stack was to live for another twenty years and was one of the last clergymen in the Church of Ireland to hold the commission of the peace in his country.

Continuity in the parochial sphere had been assured by the financial arrangements made at the time of disestablishment, though, of course, a degree of change was inevitable. During the 1870s there was a considerable number of parochial amalgamations, with the result that by 1880 there were only about 1,300 parochial units, 13 per cent fewer than there had been in 1870. There had been indeed in the three northern dioceses, Clogher, and the united dioceses of Derry and Raphoe, Down and Connor and Dromore, a small increase of parishes amounting to something over twenty in all. But Limerick, Ossory, Ferns and Leighlin, and Cashel and Emly, Waterford and Lismore had lost at least 30 per cent of their parishes by amalgamations and Cork lost nearly 25 per cent. But the process of amalgamation was checked by one factor – distance. So long as the Church of Ireland aimed at maintaining a parochial system covering the whole country, a parish could not cover a larger area than could be worked by a clergyman driving a trap.

Alterations in the parochial framework were accompanied by

considerable changes in clerical remuneration. Naturally there was a tendency towards rationalizing and standardizing incomes, but since there were a number of different diocesan schemes and since some parishes retained endowments, or had unusually productive glebes or some other special source of income, there were considerable variations in incumbents' incomes. The national average for an incumbent's income in 1900 seems to have been £265 – a slight improvement on pre-disestablishment conditions. Between the dioceses there were considerable variations, the highest average being reached in Dublin (£408) and Cloyne (£343), the lowest in Clogher (£201) and Ardagh (£181). The Dublin figures can be partly explained by the fact that in that diocese nearly twenty livings were worth over £600 per annum (one of over £900 and three others of over £800). At the other extreme there were about 320 livings, over a quarter of the total number of livings, with incomes of less than £200 per annum. At this time the average salary of a protestant secondary school master was under £100 per annum and second division clerks in government departments received £70 to £250 per annum; and the salaries of first-class clerks ranged from £200 to £650.[3]

Another change in the use of clerical man-power followed disestablishment. The number of curates fell drastically after 1871. By 1880 there were only 350; by 1914 only 290; by 1925 the total had fallen to about 200 (only in the united diocese of Down and Connor and Dromore was there, between 1871 and 1925, an increase in the number of curates employed – from about 50 to 70). And after disestablishment the easy-going incumbent who left most of his work to his curate was almost eliminated, curates being usually employed only in parishes where there was a comparatively large Church of Ireland population.

There were a number of these parishes in urban areas all over the country and in the north. But in the south and west there were a number of parishes in which there was bound to be clerical under-employment. A Cork rector with, in his son's phrase, 'a large parish in the geographical sense', had only about one hundred parishioners, and 'as a flock they did not provide much work, for it was a point of honour among them to attend church regularly, and they positively disliked being visited except in illness, when they regarded it as part of the medical treatment'.[4] At the beginning of the new century, archdeacon Healy, an experienced ecclesiastical administrator, asked how was a clergyman to devote all his energies to the work of the ministry when his whole cure consisted of about twenty families with 'no young men to form a Y.M.C.A., no lads to form a Church Lads' Brigade, even perhaps no children for a Sunday school'. It could, of course, be said, Healy added, what about study? 'But leisure itself', he replied, 'only makes a book-worm, which is very different indeed from a scholar.' Healy then lists the outlets open to an energetic man – lawn tennis, croquet, or even ping-pong, farming, gardening, rose-growing.[5] Ten years later Hannay, the rector of Westport, painted a more idealized picture of an incumbent with very few parishioners when he described 'Harold Burnaby', 'a really good man', living on a small stipend in a remote rectory in the west with forty scattered souls to look after. Burnaby not only cared for his own people, but helped all his neighbours, writing applica-tions for old age pensions and trying to find situations for those seeking employment. 'It is quite astonishing', Hannay remarks, 'how few people in the West of Ireland seem able to do anything for themselves.' Burnaby, in his obscure poverty, had 'love enough, work enough and faith enough'. He and his wife, Hannay drives home, made an important contribution to Ireland. They brought up a fine family, 'more or less of the same type. They tell the truth. They have an instinct for duty. They say their prayers. They get through a lot of work. . . . The little rectory has been, several times since it was built, a school of character of a prosaic but sound kind.'[6]

But there were Church of Ireland parishes where the work was heavy. In the north there were rural or semi-rural parishes with congregations over a thousand strong. And in Dublin, Frederick Wynne (the first professor of pastoral theology in Trinity) in St Matthias's parish between 1871 and 1893 was able to exemplify later Victorian ideals of parish work. Brought up in a county Wexford rectory on *The Christian year* and Manning's sermons, Wynne developed into a liberal evangelical (a friend once described him as 'a broad churchman with unction') and he maintained the pulpit tradition of St Matthias's, his idea of preaching being 'earnest conversation'. Wynne also laid great stress on visiting. He himself and his curates made regular house to house 'visitations', and he had a number of lay assistants, district visitors and temperance workers. He was particularly anxious that the sick should be visited, he himself taking the infectious cases. And he had the great gift of never appearing to be in a hurry. He also managed a great number of parish organizations including a band of hope, a girls' friendly society, a class for Sunday school teachers, and a ladies' theological class which had connected with it a ladies' literary society. He conducted bible classes in institutions for training domestic servants and a special service on Sunday for women discharged from prison. Divinity students were encouraged to come to his house on Sunday for tea and music round the piano in the drawing room, Wynne (who thought 'there was a great need for gentlemen in the Irish church') thoroughly believing 'in the civilizing and thus indirectly Christianizing influence of a family circle of ladies' society'.[7]

It was in the Belfast area that the Church of Ireland faced its most striking challenge. One of the most impressive phenomena in nineteenth-century Irish history was the growth of Belfast. With shipbuilding and linen as its major industries, Belfast developed rapidly into a great manufacturing centre, a major concentration of economic power. As the century progressed, the shipyards with their high gantries expanded, the port was improved, and factories with tall, slim chimneys sprang up, surrounded by networks of red brick houses, spreading in straight streets over the flat plain of the lower Lagan valley. At the beginning of the nineteenth century Belfast had about 20,000 inhabitants; by 1851 the population had more than trebled, amounting to 87,000; by 1911 it had more than quadrupled, having risen to 387,000. This rapid population increase was bound to create problems for the Church of Ireland, problems accentuated by the fact that, as the population of Belfast grew, the proportion of episcopalians in the area increased. In 1861 the members of the Church of Ireland formed just under a quarter (24·6 per cent) of the population of Belfast. In 1911 they amounted to almost one-third (30·54 per cent). Numerically speaking there were in 1861 in Belfast 30,000 episcopalians, in 1911 there were 118,000.

Obviously this large and rapid increase in the Church of

Ireland population in Belfast created an imperative demand for more parish churches and clergy, and from about 1830 the church was endeavouring to cope with the Belfast problem. In that year there were in Belfast three parish churches, St Anne's, St George's, and across the river, the small church in Bally-macarrett. During the next thirty years seven new parish churches were built. Then, in November 1862 at a meeting held in Messrs Ewart's office with Charles Lanyon in the chair, the Belfast extension and endowment society was formed. During the meeting it was mentioned that the ecclesiastical commissioners were going to receive a considerable access of income as a result of primate Beresford's death and it was therefore decided to send a deputation to Dublin to put the facts of the Belfast situation before the commissioners. No time was wasted. The deputation left Belfast that evening and had a satisfactory meeting with the commissioners.[8] During the following fifteen years eleven new parish churches were built and by 1914 Belfast was divided into thirty-four parishes with thirty-seven churches.

The great majority of these churches were, as was to be expected, Victorian Gothic buildings – erected, it need scarcely be added, usually with strict regard for cost. Some indeed were not lacking in quality, for instance St Thomas's, a graceful church on a commanding rise, or St Patrick's, Ballymacarrett, a large church capable of holding 2,000 with a 'noble tower resembling that of Magdalene at Oxford'. Gothic revivalism, so easily criticized, justified itself in Belfast by importing a novel and inspiring note into areas covered with drab, utilitarian houses and shops. Of the Belfast churches by far the most impressive in conception was St Anne's cathedral, begun in 1899 on the site of the eighteenth-century parish church. From 1895 O'Hara, the vicar of Belfast, had been urging that a cathedral should be erected in Belfast, offering himself a subscription of £1,000 towards the cost. And in 1899 the general synod, on the grounds that Belfast had become 'a noted and populous city', provided that St Anne's should be both a cathedral and a parish church, with a dean and a chapter composed of the deans and chapters of the three cathedrals of Down, Connor and Dromore. The architects, Drew and Lynn, at first proposed to erect a great Gothic church, but they had to modify their plans, and the design finally chosen was for a Romanesque building with an imposing west front.[9]

St Anne's cathedral symbolized both the growing importance of the Church of Ireland in Belfast and the increasing importance of Belfast in the Church of Ireland. Less happily perhaps, its slow progress symbolized the constant strain the church was working under in the Belfast area. When all that was done by the Church of Ireland in Belfast between 1830 and 1914 – the building of churches, parochial halls, schools and rectories, the provision which was made for stipends, the formation of church societies – is taken into account, it represents a considerable achievement. Nevertheless the position was by no means satisfactory. In Belfast the machinery of the Church of Ireland was always stretched to breaking point and resources continually lagged behind demands. In 1898 for instance, when there were about 92,000 episcopalians in Belfast, there were sittings for only 21,000. By 1914 there were only between sixty and seventy Church of Ireland parochial clergymen working in Belfast, some parishes were seriously understaffed, and many incumbents had to devote time and energy to dealing with the financial difficulties created by urgently needed building programmes. It is significant that it could be said that at the end of the nineteenth century there were only a dozen Belfast parishes in all where church people were visited by their clergy. In other parishes visiting was limited to seat-holders and subscribers. In the late 1880s, when the Belfast problem aroused acute attention, it was pointed out that visiting in Belfast was especially difficult because working men were at home only in the evening. It was also pointed out that many of the immigrants into Belfast belonged to 'less well-to-do families', which were not churchgoers in the country. 'Multitudes', a Belfast rector wrote,

refused to come to church because they have not what they considered respectable clothing, many more got into the habit of absenting themselves because they 'have nowhere to sit', and others because they do not like the service and find the forms which seem to us so decorous and stately, to be uninteresting and irksome.

In 1887 it was estimated by the archdeacon of Connor, who does not appear to have wanted to exaggerate the situation, that one-fifth of the members of the Church of Ireland in Belfast were non-churchgoers. A great urban clergyman, Roe, the energetic and autocratic rector of Ballymacarrett, tackled the problem of non-churchgoing by introducing into his parish 'the cottage lecture system'. That is to say, on weekdays he or his curate would hold a service or lecture in a conveniently situated private house. People were urged to come in their ordinary clothes, because of 'the old deeply-rooted difficulty about dress' which meant that 'a church was left to the well-to-do and more respectable classes whose clothes on Sunday would bear the test of a public inspection'.[10] But it might be added that there were social factors which told in favour of churchgoing in Belfast. Early in the twentieth century, a journalist noted for his well-informed facetiousness, writing about St Peter's, a large sub-urban church, referred to the 'men who have arrived at that interesting part of their career when attendance at public worship is absolutely necessary'.[11]

In the years following disestablishment, outside the Belfast area few new churches were built. After all, the established church was liberally – indeed in some areas over-liberally – supplied with ecclesiastical buildings. Even so, there were a few new churches such as St Kevin's on the South Circular Road, Dublin (1888), St Luke's, Cork, rebuilt in the 'North Italian Romanesque' style (1873), the 'early Celtic' church at Crosshaven (1873), the large abbey church at Bangor (1880), another large church, St Saviour's at Arklow (1899), built by Lord Carysfort, and the new church at Millicent (1883) built by Cooke-Trench, a cousin of the archbishop of Dublin. Trench, a public-spirited landlord who was a strong high churchman, provided the money required for replacing the old 'mean and unworthy' parish church by a new building by selling his hunters, shutting up half his house and reducing the garden staff. The new church, built in the Hiberno-Romanesque style had an interior lavishly decorated with marble and alabaster and ornamented with *cloisonné* work.[12] In addition, numerous churches were enlarged, renovated and redecorated. Organs were moved, lecterns, pulpits, and memorial windows erected, and the old box pews and heavy pulpits swept away. And whatever criticisms may be levelled against the taste of late Victorian church furnishings, they certainly evinced a generous determination on the part of church people to beautify the buildings which meant so much in their lives.

In 1871 a cathedral was being built in Cork, it having been decided to replace the undistinguished eighteenth-century cathedral by a new building. Burges, the architect, had to face the problem of building a church impressive enough to be a fitting cathedral for a thriving city, and yet of a size commensurate with the numbers and resources of the Church of Ireland population of the diocese. He solved his problem successfully by building in the French Renaissance style a church of unusual proportions – its height being 68 feet to a length of 168 feet – and St Finbarr's with its tall roof and three clustering spires takes full advantage of its lofty site. In the year of disestablishment, Roe, a leading Dublin distiller, approached the archbishop of Dublin with a welcome offer to restore Christ Church cathedral, then in a seriously decayed condition, and almost immediately after offering to restore the cathedral he added that he was prepared to pay for the building of a hall to house the general synod on an adjacent site. Street, the well-known architect, an enthusiastic high churchman and keen medievalist, was appointed to carry out the restoration and design the new hall which he connected to the cathedral by a covered bridge. He carried out the restoration of Christ Church in a reverend but somewhat drastic fashion, striving to recreate the cathedral on the lines visualized by its twelfth- and thirteenth-century builders.[13] As might be expected, his work was vigorously attacked on theological grounds, the protestant defence association of Ireland issuing a remonstrance against 'pictures, crosses, rood screens and other paraphernalia of the Church of Rome' and 'symbols of idolatry' being permitted in Christ Church 'under the flimsy guise of architectural adornment'. And high churchmen bitterly reflected that Roe was not elected to the general synod and so never sat in the hall he had built.[14]

Street was also consulted about the restoration of St Brigid's cathedral, Kildare, which was finally completed in 1896, and during the last thirty years of the century important improvements were carried out in at least ten other cathedrals. In three – Derry, Connor and Dromore – a chancel was added, and in Derry cathedral in addition an elaborate reredos of Caen stone with red marble column, carved oak stalls, a brass altar rail and two brass gas standards were erected. In Waterford cathedral the old galleries were swept away, an apse was added to Elphin cathedral and the rebuilding of Tuam cathedral, begun in 1861, was completed, with the result that a massive Gothic building in red sandstone was tacked on to the bleak, old seventeenth-century cathedral, which was turned into a chapter house and library.[15]

Architectural change was bound to have some influence on the conduct of public worship. A Gothicized church imperceptibly calls for heightened ceremonial. At disestablishment a determined effort had been made to stereotype by canon and rubric the ritual of the Church of Ireland, fixing it firmly in mid-nineteenth-century moulds. But during the next few decades modifications were made, cross-channel customs spread to Irish churches and twenty years after disestablishment the *Irish ecclesiastical gazette*, which had a distinctly high church bias, complacently listed a number of recent innovations – 'three-deckers swept away, the black gown well nigh altogether abolished, the holy communion more frequently celebrated, the psalms chanted, the holy days of the Church better observed, public worship more reverently conducted – all these and other more important advances'.[16]

The intellectual life of the church after disestablishment was, as in the past, greatly influenced by the Trinity divinity school, which continued to be the principal training school for its clergy. Admittedly, disestablishment had important repercussions in Trinity College. As late as 1867, when Fawcett asked the house of commons to resolve that fellowships and scholarships in Trinity should be free from religious tests, Lefroy, the senior MP for the university, emphasized that Trinity was founded 'avowedly upon protestant principles'. The following year, when the question was again impending, the board, on behalf of the fellows and scholars, petitioned parliament against 'the organic changes' which it was proposed to make. But the college attitude on this important issue changed in 1869. After disestablishment, it was agreed that it was impossible to permit the members of the Church of Ireland to retain a privileged position in the university. Moreover, Trinity and episcopalian opinion were coming round to favour united higher education. To a minority, which still possessed considerable influence and great intellectual self-confidence, the united education of protestants and catholics in Trinity was definitely preferable to encouraging the development of university education on denominational lines, which would almost certainly involve the foundation of a state-subsidized catholic institution which would probably prove a formidable competitor to Trinity. So when, in 1870, Fawcett for the third time brought forward his motion, he was seconded by Plunket, one of the Trinity MPs, who in the course of his speech emphasized that his constituents supported 'the great principle of united education' and were anxious 'to repel . . . the aggression of ultramontane ambition which threatened their university'.[17] In 1873, by the measure usually known as 'Fawcett's act', all religious tests were abolished in the university of Dublin and Trinity College, except in respect of professorships and lectureships in the divinity school. From then on Trinity was legally an undenominational university and there was the possibility that some time in the future the divinity school might come under the control of a board, a majority of whose members would be neither clergymen nor episcopalians. Admittedly, as the board pointed out in 1880, this situation could not arise for at least a quarter of a century. Nevertheless the danger existed, and members of the Church of Ireland were all the more conscious of it when they saw that the Roman catholics and presbyterians each controlled a divinity school, endowed partly as a result of the Irish church act. In 1876 the Trinity board, by five votes to three, decided that the control of the divinity school might be transferred to a council appointed by the Church of Ireland, and in 1879 Lord Belmore introduced in the lords a bill which he hoped would settle the question. The divinity school (Ireland) bill provided that the control of the divinity school should be transferred to the representative church body. The college was to make to the representative church body an annual payment equal to the salaries in the school at the time of transfer – a payment which could be commuted for a lump sum. The school was to have the use of lecture-rooms in college, and students on the books of college were not to be charged. This bill aroused intense opposition. At a largely attended meeting of the university senate – it was said that about one hundred members of the senate had qualified for the purpose of being present – Carson, a well-known clerical fellow, moved a resolution strongly condemning the bill. He wanted the school to be controlled by the college through a board of theological studies, the members of which would be members of the Church of Ireland (Carson, in a magnificent archaism, in fact spoke of them as being members of the Church of England). Salmon, who was strongly opposed to 'a protestant Maynooth', managed to carry an amendment which implied that the senate would support the compromise solution which he had been advocating – that the divinity school be controlled by a council nominated partly by the college and partly by the church.

Belmore withdrew his bill, and at the close of the year the board and the bench met in the archbishop of Dublin's palace in St Stephen's Green. The board's attitude seems to have been hardening – it was pointed out that much of the work of the divinity school was done for the Church of England and the colonial churches. Nevertheless agreement was reached on all points but one. The bishops proposed that professors and lecturers in the divinity school should be nominated by the bench and appointed by the board. The board would not accept this suggestion and the discussions lapsed. During the next twenty years the situation remained unchanged. The board continued to be composed of members of the Church of Ireland and Salmon became provost in 1888, so there was no immediate reason for the Church of Ireland to be alarmed. But when in the early years of the twentieth century the Irish university question was being vigorously debated, the bishops in 1903 again asked the board to discuss the method by which divinity professors should be selected. The board replied by pointing out that 'whether the members of the board be devout members of the Church or not, they are honest men' and would be bound to select teachers of divinity who would have the confidence of the church. The bishops were not satisfied and in 1906 the general synod set up a committee to present the Church of Ireland's case on the divinity school issue before the royal commission on Trinity College. In a statement which it drew up this committee emphasized that the Church of Ireland wished the connection between the university and the church to be maintained. 'Without a theological faculty', the committee stated, 'a university is without one of its most effective instruments of culture.'

At the same time it was of the greatest advantage to the church 'that it should have a learned clergy who have received a liberal education along with laymen in the free atmosphere of a great university'. The committee went on to urge that the control of the divinity school should be entrusted to an academic body composed of persons in communion with the Church of Ireland, including some members of the episcopal bench. This solution of the divinity school question was recommended by the royal commission in its report and adopted in 1911, the king's letter of that year laying down that the divinity school be governed (subject to the control of the board) by a council composed of six members of the board, all of whom were to be members of the Church of Ireland, three members of the teaching staff of the school and three bishops nominated by the bench of bishops.

The intellectual climate of the school changed slowly. When Salmon became provost in 1888 he was succeeded as regius professor by John Gwynn, a scholar of great linguistic gifts (he was said to have learned Syriac 'to relieve the tedium of long railway journeys from Donegal to Dublin') and a man of great kindliness and fine courtesy. But he was not outstanding as a lecturer (in his obituary it was stressed that 'it was outside the lecture room that the teacher was at his best')[18] and the dominant influence in the school was Salmon's pupil and friend John Henry Bernard, who became archbishop King's lecturer in succession to Gwynn in 1888. Bernard's scholarship was impressive in range and quality, he could express himself with lucidity and when needs be with pungent force, and he soon showed that he was not only a scholar but an able administrator and a man of affairs, sensitive, outspoken, persuasive and decisive. He was concerned to preserve the Church of Ireland from isolation, eager at the beginning of the new century that it have 'a larger, a more hopeful, more catholic view of the faith than common thirty years ago'. He had a cautious appreciation of contemporary trends in biblical criticism, and his profound loyalty to the church as an institution, together with his instinctive respect for order and decorum, gave him a sympathetic bias towards many aspects of English high churchmanship. As a teacher he was most impressive. At the outset of his career, he was described as having 'the appearance and temperament of an undergraduate, an undergraduate raised to a higher power',[19]

and he placed his stamp – of solid, balanced, cautious comprehensiveness, impregnated with intense pride in the anglican
tradition – on the divinity school and the church at large.

Before disestablishment the numbers in the divinity school
were relatively high, it being estimated that in the period
1858–67 the number of students securing the divinity testimonium was almost exactly one-third of those graduating in
arts. With disestablishment the numbers in the divinity school
fell abruptly but they rose again in the 1880s, reaching a maximum in the mid-1890s when they again began to decline.
Bernard attributed this latter fall to two factors, 'a large cause
which applies to other parts of the world' and which had
affected Ireland rather later than England, and 'the feeling on
the part of Churchmen that Trinity is becoming more and more
secular' (it is doubtful this feeling was widespread; it certainly
did not prevent nearly all the candidates in the Church of
Ireland coming to Trinity during the following fifty years).
The early decline in numbers in the divinity school may be
partly explained by the fact that in the years following disestablishment a number of men were ordained for Irish dioceses
who had not secured the testimonium. This situation soon
changed, and in the twentieth century it was rare for Trinity
College, Dublin, graduates in orders in the Church of Ireland
not to have the testimonium – and at the beginning of the
century 84 per cent of the Church of Ireland clergy were TCD
graduates. It may be added that a high proportion of the Trinity,
Dublin men in orders – about 45 per cent – were working in
England or overseas, and between 1873 and 1913 1,044 Trinity,
Dublin graduates were ordained for English dioceses. Admittedly
this was only 3·6 per cent of the total English ordinations, but
when the size of the Church of Ireland is taken into account its
contribution is impressive. Bernard, however, was not altogether
happy about the divinity school. It was not, he explained to the
royal commission of 1906 on Trinity College, 'altogether a good
thing to try and combine the two functions of a school of scientific theology and a training college for Church of Ireland clergymen in one institution'. But he was afraid that one reason made
this combination necessary, 'the poverty of our men'. In
Bernard's opinion if the divinity school was separated from the
university a number of men would be ordained without having

taken a degree. A step towards solving the problems raised by
Bernard was taken in 1913 when the Church of Ireland divinity
hostel was founded. Occupying two houses in Mountjoy Square,
it provided accommodation for about twenty-five students, and
it was stressed that it was to be regarded not merely as 'a
respectable lodging house, but as a home for Christian culture
and serious study'.[20]

The divinity school was undoubtedly a great unifying and
sobering force in the Church of Ireland. As has been said, it gave
the clergy a common intellectual background, and an outstanding element in its ethos was a cautious distaste for extremes.
This was one reason why, at a time when the Church of England
was sorely distressed by ritual disputes, often reflecting grave
differences of doctrinal emphasis, the Church of Ireland was not
seriously disturbed by controversy over either doctrine or
ceremonial. Another reason for this was the legislation passed
during the early 1870s. The post-disestablishment canons left
few opportunities for advanced or even moderate ritualists to
depart from established usage, and this deprived the anti-
ritualists of satisfactory targets. Again, the ecclesiastical courts
had indubitably been created by the church and derived their
authority from it. Thus their jurisdiction seemed to be un-
challengeable. Of the cases which were heard by the court of
the general synod between 1871 and 1914, only three involved
matters of doctrine or ritual. The only 'big case' in this category
arose in 1892 when there was an appeal to the court from the
Dublin diocesan court, which had dismissed a complaint against
the erection in St Bartholomew's of 'a brass or gilt cross' on a
wooden tripod behind the communion table. The court of the
general synod (the archbishop of Armagh, Knox, and the
bishop of Derry, Alexander, dissenting) allowed the appeal. Mr
Justice Holmes, delivering judgment, emphasized that the court
had confined itself to subjecting the language used in canon
thirty-six 'to a critical analysis which must appear cold and
unsympathetic to those who feel strongly on the subject'. The
cross was immediately removed and shortly afterwards placed
on a stand in front of the communion table.

Each of the two doctrinal cases to come before the court of
the general synod possessed elements of the absurd. A clergyman in the diocese of Down, attacking archbishop Plunket of

Dublin for his action in respect of the reformed episcopal church in Spain, became involved in a newspaper controversy in which he appeared 'to uphold and affirm the sacrifice of the mass'. The court found him guilty, adding that he had used language 'unbecoming a clergyman'. He retracted and shortly afterwards 'the bishop and some of the wealthy laymen bought him out and he disappeared'. About the same time 'a rather eccentric' clergyman in the diocese of Limerick was found guilty of attacking the practice of infant baptism and refusing to wear a surplice when performing divine service.[21]

The records of the court of the general synod certainly do not suggest that ritualism was a serious problem in the Church of Ireland. Nevertheless there were low churchmen who were greatly afraid that it might work its way into Ireland, and they were quick to denounce any practice which they thought had dangerous implications. To elevate the paten and cup, it was pointed out, 'even as high as the breast', with the purpose of indicating a sacrificial act, was contrary to the canons. About 1890 all the professors in the divinity school (with one exception) were said to be high churchmen. It was rumoured (quite erroneously) that a guild had been formed in Trinity on the basis of compulsory celibacy and compulsory confession. Ritualism, it was asserted, was becoming fashionable:[22]

The nobles and grandees learned to like it when over in London for the season. On their return they set the fashion. They influence the clergy, and even the bishops, now of a rank more likely to be affected by the smiles and favours of the great.

At the end of the 1880s the protestant defence association drew archbishop Plunket's attention to the way in which public worship was being conducted in two churches in the diocese of Dublin, St Bartholomew's and Grangegorman. Plunket temperately but firmly replied 'that within the comprehensive limits of any church which claims as ours a national character large room must be left for the exercise of private judgement'. Knox, the primate, the following year expressed himself more bluntly, vigorously condemning the narrow-mindedness which arrogated to itself the sole privilege of defining what was right and what was wrong, and he strongly criticized attempts 'to coerce and denounce certain incumbents and congregations, simply because they do not carry on their services with the same dull, solemn monotony which delights and no doubt edifies many'. A few years later he referred to the protestant defence association as 'really a protestant disturbance society', which sent 'emissaries – a polite word for spies – to sow discord in parishes'.[23]

In 1895 indignant protests were made when it was heard that a few well-known high churchmen, including Gore and Dolling, were to speak at a Church of Ireland congress to be held in the diocese of Derry, and after a two-day debate in the general synod the proposal to hold the congress was abandoned. In 1900 the cross in front of the communion table in St Bartholomew's was surreptitiously removed and a large meeting at the Rotunda requested Peacocke, Plunket's successor as archbishop of Dublin, not to permit it to be replaced. The archbishop refused to defer to this request, pointing out that when the cross had been erected all legal requirements had been met. St John's, Sandymount (a trustee church) was, at the beginning of the new century, strongly criticized in the Dublin diocesan synod, being regarded as the centre of the most extreme high churchmanship in Ireland. The dean of St Patrick's, Bernard, countered these attacks by pointing out that, if illegalities were being committed in the conduct of divine worship in St John's, charges should be brought in the ecclesiastical courts.[24] No legal action was taken, but in 1910 police had to be brought in to check brawling in the church. There was trouble also in Belfast. The more extreme Belfast protestants had become critical of the unionist government's attitude to Roman catholicism and ritualism and in 1902 the official unionist candidate for south Belfast, Dunbar-Buller, a member of the general synod, was defeated by Sloan, an independent unionist, and a leading member of the Belfast protestant association. One of Sloan's supporters, Trew, a linen worker, who was said to be a methodist preacher, at open-air meetings denounced St Clement's and St George's. There were stormy scenes in St Clement's, the brawlers objecting to the use of *Hymns ancient and modern*, and the incumbent, the Rev. William Peoples, had to be escorted between the church and his home by a large force of police. In the end the church was closed for a time and Peoples left the diocese. And St George's, a church in the city centre noted for the ceremonial dignity (within the rules of the Church of Ireland) with which its services were conducted, had to be protected by the police against angry mobs.[25]

But extreme protestants protested vainly against the tendencies of the time. In England, as the nineteenth century drew towards its close, it was clear that both the high church and the broad church movements had significantly influenced that great body of churchmen who could be described as moderate anglicans. With the Church of Ireland deriving most of its intellectual subsistence from England – readers of the *Irish ecclesiastical gazette* and its successor the *Church of Ireland gazette* were kept in continuous touch with English theological scholarship – what would be termed central churchmanship in England (itself continually undergoing modification and readjustment to contemporary trends) was bound to have considerable influence over the Church of Ireland, and almost imperceptibly to shape its ideas and pattern of ecclesiastical life. But the Church of Ireland, a small, homogeneous church, with strong, simple loyalties, set in a slowly changing rural community with its own difficulties, was to some extent insulated from the pressures which during the later nineteenth century affected the churches of England and Scotland. The piety it nourished was often deep; its spirit was not very venturesome; it did not require to be. And it is of some significance that six outstanding churchmen brought up in the Church of Ireland, Charles, the distinguished Old Testament scholar, a broad churchman, Dolling, the high church slum parson, Lilley, a leader of anglican modernism, Maturin, the great Roman catholic preacher, Edward Dowden, bishop of Edinburgh, a high churchman, and the Jesuit Father Tyrrell, a daring thinker and pungent controversialist, all made their careers outside Ireland.

Nevertheless the Church of Ireland shared in the powerful movements which were sweeping through the Christian church towards the close of the nineteenth century. There was a growing feeling that there should be an earnest and sustained effort to attain Christian unity; missionary activity was ever extending, making incessant demands on the home churches and offering them a continuous stimulus; and there was an increasing concern with social questions. In 1899 Paterson Smyth, the rector of St Anne's, Dublin, seconded by the bishop of Ossory, persuaded the general synod to set up a committee (subsequently known as the social service committee) to consider 'the improvement of the social and domestic condition of life amongst the poor'. In its first report this committee suggested that parish committees should be set up to deal with social subjects from the Christian point of view. These committees, not knowing where to get the information they wanted, soon 'became perplexed and in danger of losing interest in the movement', so the social service committee prepared a social service handbook for Ireland (edited by Paterson Smyth), containing articles with bibliographies on 'the more pressing questions' – old age pensions, industrial schools, housing of the poor and the 'drink question'. The book sold slowly and in 1902 the committee felt 'there was a most discouraging lack of interest in the study of social questions in Ireland'.[26]

But a certain amount was accomplished. In 1907 the social service committee held a conference of representatives of philanthropic societies connected with the Church of Ireland. A pamphlet was produced clearly stating how the public could co-operate in the administration of the children's act of 1908. In Belfast sermons were preached on the importance of providing open spaces for city children and 'the bishop's workingmen's committee' set up to study social questions. In Dublin some parishes established bursaries for elderly ladies. A drive was made, led by Christ Church, Leeson Park, to effect improvements in poor law administration and in 1906 successful efforts were made in a few Dublin districts to return poor law guardians pledged to workhouse reform. Naturally enough in Dublin, a city with large areas of tenement dwellings, often in a decaying state, attention to the housing question aroused the disturbed attention of the social service committee, and the parish of St Mathias set up a small company which took a tenement house, its aim being to spend all its profits (after paying 4 per cent to its shareholders) on improving the property or purchasing further houses.

The social service committee was not reappointed in 1912, the reason possibly being that some of its work was being performed by the committee appointed to co-operate with the Irish presbyterian church – an off-shoot of the home reunion committee set up by the general synod in 1905 to promote spiritual and organic union between the various religious denominations in Ireland which had so much belief and interests in common. This committee, a few years after its appointment, candidly stated that its work was 'mainly one of quiet observation'. It reported extensively on reunion activities outside Ireland, but kept in mind that the 'Lambeth quadrilateral' 'has a force which is at once stimulative and restrictive'. The 'restrictive' aspect came to the fore in 1913 when the board of Trinity College, acting in provost Traill's phrase as 'the owners' of the college chapel, allowed a presbyterian service to be held in the building. The regius professor of divinity and the archbishop of Armagh both protested, the latter declaring that this action was likely to 'throw back indefinitely the cause of home reunion'.[27] However the home reunion committee was much impressed by the proceedings of the great world-wide missionary conference held in Edinburgh in 1910. In 1911 an annual 'day of intercession for unity' was appointed by the bishops, and the Church of Ireland played its part in preparatory work for the conference on faith and order which it was hoped to hold in the near future.

At home in Ireland in 1908 a conference was held between the board of education of the general synod and the elementary education committee of the general assembly, and three years later, in 1911, the general synod appointed a committee to co-operate with a committee of the general assembly in philanthropic and religious work.[28] The issues which the two committees tackled over the next three years were temperance, industrial schools and the *Ne Temere* decree. Some years later the joint committee appointed by the general synod and the general assembly advocated, as a wartime measure, restrictions on the consumption of alcohol. In 1915 the joint committees supported a letter to the prime minister signed by cardinal Logue, the archbishop of Armagh, the moderator of the general assembly and the vice-president of the methodist conference, demanding that steps should be taken against 'the drink traffic'. In the following year the committees endeavoured to secure that the operations of the board of control for the liquor trade should be extended to Ireland. Arrangements were made for deputations from the committee to meet the lord lieutenant when he visited Belfast on 28 April 1916. But the visit had to be postponed, and when some time later it was suggested that a deputation from the committee should meet the lord lieutenant, he replied that as 'the question' of extending the sphere of the central board 'was one of general policy' no useful purpose would be attained by his meeting the deputation. The committee then declared that 'widespread disappointment had been aroused by the refusal of the authorities to carry out in Ireland reforms which had been successful in many places in Great Britain', and the Irish unionist party informed the committee that it would support any measure for the restriction of the drink traffic introduced by the government.[29] But the government, with discontent widespread in Ireland, understandably abstained from dealing with an issue on which action was bound to produce vehement controversy. In 1920 the committee endorsed the suggestion that a united temperance council of the Christian churches should be constituted and the following year it regretted that 'owing to the political situation' it could not start a propaganda campaign in favour of the six-point programme approved by the temperance council. It may be added that the committee also strove to educate public opinion on 'the very painful but urgently important subject of venereal disease', and also pressed hard for higher salaries for secondary and primary school teachers.

The movement towards Christian reunion, which was growing in significance from the beginning of the twentieth century, derived much of its impetus from missionary experience in non-Christian areas. During the nineteenth century there was a great expansion on a world-wide front of Christian missionary effort. In this the Church of Ireland had its share. Long before disestablishment, Irish churchmen were working overseas. Among them were Charles Inglis, bishop of Nova Scotia, the first anglican colonial bishop; Travers Lewis, consecrated bishop of Ontario in 1861, and later metropolitan of Canada; Alexander Garrett, who worked for years amongst the Indians of Vancouver, for whom he translated a portion of the prayer book into Chinook; and John Bowen, appointed bishop of Sierra Leone in 1857. In 1881 the general synod appointed a board of missions which published annual statistics showing financial support given by the Church of Ireland to the missionary societies, the CMS, the SPG, the colonial and continental church society, the South African mission and the society for promoting Christianity among the Jews.

The appointment of the board of missions was a sign of the interest which was being taken in work overseas. In 1885 Trinity was affected by the wave of evangelicalism which was sweeping through the British universities. A series of meetings was held in the Regent House, culminating in a 'striking scene' when forty men came forward, prepared to serve 'wherever the way might be made clear'. Shortly afterwards the Dublin university mission to Fuh Kien, a coastal province of China, south of Formosa, was started. A Trinity man, the Rev. W. H. Collins, who was a qualified surgeon, had been working there a quarter of a century earlier, and his son, J. S. Collins, curate of Birr, was the first Trinity man to volunteer for service with the new mission. Another Trinity graduate, Robert Stewart, was already working in the area. Stewart was acutely aware of the disadvantages under which illiterate catechists laboured when working among the Chinese, and he emphasized the importance of education, founding village schools whose brighter pupils would attend the high school of Foochow. The Fuh Kien mission, threatened by resurgent Chinese nationalism, went through perilous days, and in 1895 Stewart, his wife and six other missionaries were killed by 'the vegetarians', an anti-foreign association. But the mission continued and in 1912 Trinity College, Foochow, a high school with impressive buildings, was opened. In 1952 the title of the mission was changed to the 'Far Eastern mission', since it was no longer functioning in China proper, but was assisting missionaries working in Malaya and Singapore.[30] In 1890, five years after the Trinity College Fuh Kien mission was started, the SPG was informed that several Trinity men were prepared to volunteer for work in any region selected by the society, on condition they were permitted to work as a community. The offer was accepted, and the mission, consisting at first of five men and one woman, was settled at Hazaribagh in Chota Nagpur where it set up a dispensary, a hospital and a little later a school.[31]

About the time the two missions were founded an Irishman, George Pilkington, was helping to found the church in Uganda. Pilkington, a son of the able QC who had advised Irish churchmen at the time of disestablishment, was influenced by

93

evangelicalism when at Cambridge, and started conducting open-air meetings. In the summer of 1887 he brought over a group of Cambridge men to Ireland with the aim of holding a series of out-of-doors evangelical meetings near his home in Westmeath. The local rector, Richard Dowse, insisted that the meetings should be held in a hall, so Pilkington 'arranged accordingly for open windows and a loud voice when speaking'. In 1890 Pilkington went out to Uganda as a CMS missionary and, being a good linguist, he was asked by his bishop to translate the Bible into Luganda, a task he finished on furlough in county Westmeath. In 1897 he was killed when acting as interpreter with a small government force which was resisting Sudanese mutineers.[32]

In 1914 the Church of Ireland was able to list 266 missionaries – including six bishops – drawn from its membership.[33] The number of missionary meetings, lectures and bazaars which were held indicate that there was a keen and widespread interest in the missionary movement. This not only meant that the Church of Ireland made its contribution in men, women and money to missionary work. It also, by creating a lively and personal interest in places and people overseas, opened up new horizons to many members of the church who otherwise might have been scarcely aware of much beyond their own country or parish.

The Church of Ireland was also deeply involved in an effort to build up non-Roman catholic episcopal churches in the Iberian peninsula. In Spain and Portugal, traditionally fervently Roman catholic countries, there were, from the middle of the nineteenth century, partly as the result of the evangelizing activities of foreign churches, small groups of protestants. In time in both countries some protestant congregations came together, constituting the reformed church of Spain and the Lusitanian church, and adopted the episcopalian form of church government and a liturgy based on the prayer book but with elements from the Moza rubric and Braga rites. In 1878 these churches requested the Lambeth conference to arrange for the consecration of a bishop for them. The conference appointed a sub-committee to deal with the question, and the Irish bishops, who were approached by the Spanish and Portuguese reformed churches in the following year, decided after some deliberation to defer taking any action on the matter until after the next Lambeth conference. When it met in 1888 the assembled bishops, referring to the Iberian churches, declared that they would deprecate any action which did not 'regard primitive and established principles of jurisdiction and the interests of the whole anglican communion'. Consequently, in the following year the Irish bishops informed the Spanish and Portuguese episcopalians, who had approached them, that they could not see their way to consecrate a bishop for them.

Knox of Armagh, by no means a low churchman, must have expressed the feelings of many Irish churchmen when he wrote, 'I cannot bring myself to turn my back on any movement which results in coming out from the Church of Rome, especially in Spain, steeped in ignorance and superstition'. But the question of how the Iberian episcopalians could be helped was, as Alexander of Derry said, 'a very difficult and delicate one'. Respect for ecclesiastical jurisdiction is inherent in the episcopalian system of church government, there were long-established rules against bishops 'wandering' into dioceses with which they had no legal connection, and Magee, the bishop of Peterborough, warned his Irish friends that the consecration by Irish prelates of a bishop for Spain would sever relations between the Church of Ireland and the Church of England. On the other hand, it could be stressed that a bishop was a bishop of the whole catholic church and concerned with the well-being of every part of it. Other issues complicated the controversy. It was said the Spanish and Portuguese liturgies, compared with the book of common prayer, seemed theologically defective, omissions having been made which might have been approved by low churchmen. Finally it was pointed out that Cabrera, the Spanish protestant leader, had, after leaving the Roman catholic church, associated himself for years with presbyterian organizations.

The Spanish and Portuguese protestants had a loyal and indefatigable friend in Plunket, bishop of Meath, and after 1884 archbishop of Dublin, who travelled widely in Europe – his biographer admits that his prolonged absences from Meath aroused critical comment – and was keenly interested in continental protestantism, more especially in the small protestant communities in the Latin countries. His feelings were summed up in the lines of a hymn he quotes in 'An appeal for Spain'. It begins:

> Safe we have reached the shore,
> Praise God on high!

and continues

> Shall then our brethren sink,
> And we so near.

Reichel, Plunket's successor in Meath, when discussing the Spanish church question, remarked that Plunket had 'an amiable character and tenacity of purpose'. And if, as Reichel rather implies, the former quality rendered him gullible, his tenacity was of the greatest value to the Spanish and Portuguese protestants.

Plunket visited the peninsula, where he was greatly impressed by the courage and sincerity of the small bands of episcopal protestants whom he met, took a leading part in raising funds for the Spanish and Portuguese episcopalian churches and created an ecclesiastical sensation by ordaining in 1891 his private chaplain, Andrew Cassels, for the Lusitanian church. This aroused a storm, and the Irish bishops published a cautiously worded declaration saying that they did not feel called on to protest against the archbishop of Dublin holding ordinations on behalf of the reformers of Spain and Portugal in those countries. But Plunket was prepared to go further and at the beginning of 1894, along with the bishops of Clogher (Stack) and Down (Welland), he issued a statement to the effect that having taken account of 'the singular patience and steadfastness' of the Spanish and Portuguese protestants, they intended to consecrate a bishop for each of those churches, unless a formal protest was made by the majority of the Irish bishops or the general synod. The Irish bishops decided (Derry and Cork dissenting) that if the archbishop of Dublin and the two bishops who were prepared to act with him conferred episcopal orders on clergymen in Spain and Portugal, the Irish bench 'would not regard it as an indefensible exercise of the powers entrusted to the episcopate'. When a few months later the general synod met, a resolution heartily approving the intended consecrations was moved. After a vigorous debate a less emotionally worded resolution was substituted affirming that the synod, believing 'that such action belongs entirely to the bishops themselves in the exercise of their episcopal powers', left the matter in their hands. And in September Plunket, Stack and Welland consecrated Cabrera in Madrid.

After this consecration the Church of Ireland exercised a general oversight over the non-Roman catholic episcopalian churches in Spain and Portugal, archbishop Gregg paying four visits to the peninsula between 1924 and 1934. Cabrera died in 1916, and in 1956 the bishop of Meath and two north American bishops consecrated as his successor Santos Molina, who had spent some years in Burgos gaol after being found guilty of being a freemason, and in 1958 the bishop of Meath assisted at the consecration of a bishop for the Lusitanian church. In 1963 the Church of Ireland received the Spanish reformed church and the Lusitanian church into full communion, each church then having about ten congregations.[34]

The Irish bishops' consecration of Cabrera aroused remarkably little comment in Ireland, though a letter appeared in the *Freeman's Journal*, signed 'A citizen of Dublin', saying that the writer, being in Madrid at the time of the consecration, which had aroused no interest there, had, by the help of Cook's found Cabrera's church and discovered the small and devout congregation to be entirely composed of 'a humble class'. English high churchmen, however, in the thick of the controversy over anglican orders, were deeply disturbed by what the *Church Times* characteristically labelled 'the Spanish scandal'. Lord Halifax, the president of the English church union, wrote to the archbishop of Toledo, deploring on behalf of English 'members of the catholic church' the action of the Irish prelates. Cardinal Vaughan promptly wrote privately to the archbishop, explaining that Halifax was not a catholic but the head of 'one of the sects of the anglican church'. The archbishop of Toledo allowed a translation from the Latin of Vaughan's letter to be published in the press, and Vaughan felt constrained to write to Halifax apologizing for an offensive turn of phrase which he attributed to faulty translation.

V

THE CHURCH AND IRISH
POLITICS

~~~~~~

FORTY YEARS AFTER disestablishment a period of change and
bitter strife in Irish politics began with the introduction of the
third home rule bill in 1912. From the time home rule became a
major political issue the Church of Ireland had expressed its
opinion in no uncertain terms. A fortnight before Gladstone
introduced his first home rule bill in the house of commons, a
special meeting of the general synod was held to consider it.
'Have we, the members of this synod,' demanded the archbishop
of Dublin, who presided, 'any right to deal with a question of
politics?' 'If we distinguish politics from party', he answered, 'I
say unhesitatingly we have.' Behind the demand for home rule,
he warned the synod, 'there lurks the demand for entire separation and a very advanced form of socialism'. Answering the
argument that it might be dangerous to refuse home rule, he
asked, 'Was it right that honest Christian men should yield to
terrorists?' Besides, he believed that it would be possible by
'fair and just legislation to repress crime and at the same time to
concede the claims of justice'. After hearing this address, the
synod unanimously passed a series of resolutions protesting
against home rule. In 1893 when Gladstone introduced his
second home rule bill, the standing committee of the general
synod sent a protest against the bill to every select vestry.
Within a fortnight 1,190 out of 1,218 vestries signified their

approval of the protest, and a special meeting of the general synod sanctioned a petition to parliament against the bill, which archbishop Knox of Armagh succinctly characterized as 'a bill to suppress the protestant faith'.[1]

Of course a few members of the Church of Ireland were home rulers, including the first two leaders of the home rule party in parliament, Butt and Parnell, and the term was coined by a clergyman of the Church of Ireland, Joseph Galbraith. Galbraith's friend, William Carroll, was also a home ruler. A man of copious learning, a hard-working Dublin slum parson, a prolific pamphleteer and a vigorous advocate of Irish industrial development, he delivered in 1872 at a home rule meeting in Dundalk a very exuberant attack on the government. But Carroll, a man of ill-controlled enthusiasms, carried little weight in the councils of the church. Galbraith, a fellow of Trinity, however, had played an important part in the financial reorganization of the church in the early 1870s, making a great number of essential actuarial calculations. Full of fervent feeling, after disestablishment, 'smarting under a deep sense of wrong to Irish protestants', and influenced by his close friend, Butt, he joined the home rule movement; and in 1888 Parnell (presumably overlooking the clerical disabilities act) asked him to be a parliamentary candidate for the Stephen's Green division of Dublin. His candidature, Parnell told him, 'would tend to assuage the feelings of alarm undoubtedly existing amongst many of our protestant fellow countrymen at the prospect of home rule, and would afford another example of the spirit of toleration belonging to the bulk of Irish catholics'. But Galbraith's adherence to the home rule cause aroused considerable irritation amongst his clerical and academic colleagues. Shortly after he was asked by Parnell to stand for parliament, the primate wrote to Galbraith saying that by enrolling himself as a member of the National League he had made a very painful impression on the representative church body. The National League, the primate explained, 'had adopted a line of evident hostility to the rights of property' and the representative church body, having appointed receivers on certain estates, was in the position of a landlord. If the finance committee, the primate went on to point out, was required to discuss how to defeat the League, 'they would have to do so with a member of the league as their colleague'. He suggested that Galbraith should resign from the finance committee, and in the event Galbraith ceased to be a member of the representative church body.[2]

But the last decade of the nineteenth century not only saw defeat of Mr Gladstone's second home rule bill; it was an era marked by the beginnings of movements which were to make a great impression on Irish life and thought – the literary and Gaelic revivals, agricultural co-operation, the foundation of the united Irish league and Sinn Fein. In the vigorous stirring of Irish intellectual and artistic life which marked the turn of the century, many lay members of the Church of Ireland played a conspicuous part, and one beneficed clergyman, Hannay, the rector of Westport, came to the fore as a vigorous exponent of a fresh approach to Irish problems. Hannay might well be considered the Irish Sidney Smith. Fair-minded and alert to new ideas, he had an active and agile pen and a ready appreciation of the ridiculous. After becoming rector of Westport in 1892, he spent long evenings struggling to learn German and to get to grips with modern German theology. Early in the new century he published two works on early Christian monasticism and in 1905 he published the first of a series of novels dealing with Irish issues, and more especially with the problem of what ought to be the attitude of Irish protestants to Irish nationalism. These novels are preserved from the stiff didacticism which so often afflicts novels with a purpose by Hannay's interest in people, wide knowledge of Irish life and kindly delight in its absurdities.

Hannay was a fervent, if idiosyncratic, nationalist. 'I recognise,' he wrote in 1907, 'one loyalty as binding as a duty on me, loyalty to Ireland and to Edward VII as *de facto* and I believe *de jure* king of Ireland. I do not admit I have a duty of loyalty to England or to the empire.'[3] But unlike the great majority of Irish nationalists he was a strong anglican, very critical of the theology and ethos of Roman catholicism. In Ireland the Roman catholic church was, he thought, aggressively seeking power, while the Church of Ireland was out of touch with many vital elements in Irish life. In his first novel, by describing the ecclesiastical buildings in a small west of Ireland town, he indicates his opinion of the two churches. The Roman catholic church was obtrusively raw and self-assertive. The Church of Ireland, he wrote, 'has turned its back deliberately even osten-

tatiously, on the town. Within the locked gates that lead to it
the gravel is smoothly raked and the grass on the graves trim
and tidy.' However, it should be said at this point that Hannay,
if critical of the churches, recognized that there were in the
ranks of their clergy many men of simple goodness and spiritual
power. Hannay also, unlike most nationalists, thought that the
Irish gentry were 'by far the best class in the country'. But he
had to sadly admit that they had[4]

quite forgotten that their grandfathers stood for Irish nationality and
had chosen to call themselves English. In the future men will speak
of them as stupid and blind almost beyond belief, but no one will call
them either cowardly or base. At different stages of the struggle they
might have saved themselves and led a really united Ireland in a
great battle for nationality. They never did, and never would. They
conceived of themselves as an English garrison, and held loyalty to
England as their prime duty.

About the time he published his first novel Hannay began to
play a prominent part in the Gaelic league.[5] The first president
of the league was Douglas Hyde, the son of a Church of Ireland
rector. Hyde earnestly wanted his fellow-countrymen to build
up an Irish Ireland, and that Ireland, he was convinced, could
find and express itself only by learning and using the Irish
language, 'the tongue of the Gael'. The Gaelic league claimed
to be non-sectarian and non-political, and though the majority
of its members were catholics, protestants were made very
welcome. Indeed a leading Church of Ireland Gaelic leaguer,
T. W. Rolleston, who was a friend of Hannay, hoped that the
work of the league would undermine the power of the Roman
catholic clergy in Ireland. Irish politics, he wrote in 1905,[6]

have been like everything else absorbed into the church – everything
else but one thing, the Gaelic League. The league represents the last
effort of the Irish spirit for national and personal independence. The
church began by opposing it – it is now, as usual, doing its utmost to
absorb it.

Hannay himself in the autumn of 1906 discovered painfully
how religious and cultural were intertwined. On the grounds
that Hannay in his novels had attacked 'catholics and Irishmen
as such', the parish priest of Tuam used his position as chair-
man of the local branch of the league to prevent Hannay being

elected to the Feis committee. A number of Gaelic leaguers supported Hannay but, to avoid strife, in the end he withdrew from the executive of the league.

The non-political nature of the league is a matter of definition. It was not linked to any political party, but obviously enthusiasm for the spread of the Irish language inevitably tended to ally itself with the desire for Irish self-government. The *Church of Ireland gazette* in 1904 remarked that, though Irish protestants and unionists (it treated the two terms as practically synonymous) were prepared to assist in the preservation of the historic Irish language, they were completely unfitted by their education 'for the narrow views of life and literature that seem to be the creed of the Gaelic League'.[7] And just about a year later Stack, the bishop of Clogher, complained that, while at the beginning the Gaelic league in the north of Ireland 'was largely taken up by church people' (including Kane, the rector of Christ Church, Belfast and grand master of the Orangemen), it had 'fallen into the hands of very extreme people all (or nearly all) of one way of political thinking'.[8]

However, between 1904 and 1908 a number of letters appeared in the *Church of Ireland gazette* urging members of the church to participate in the activities of the league which, it was asserted, was revitalizing Irish intellectual life and helping to create a spirit of self-reliance and of service to Ireland. On St Patrick's day 1904 a service in Irish was held in St Kevin's, Dublin, and the following year Hannay persuaded Bernard, the dean of St Patrick's, to permit a communion service to be celebrated in Irish in the cathedral on St Patrick's day. In announcing the service, Bernard expressed the hope that none would attend 'except those who can speak or understand Irish'. Two years later three petitions with nearly 500 signatories in all, requesting a monthly service in Irish in St Patrick's were presented to Bernard. He refused to accede to this request on the grounds that such a service would be of 'no special spiritual advantage' to most of the signatories because 'they could not (in the large majority of cases) attend the service personally nor could they (in many cases) understand the service if present'.[9]

The Cumann Gaodhalach na h-Eaglaise had been formed in 1914 to express 'all those aspirations for a more intense and real national character in the church'. With a membership by 1918 of about 140, it arranged for services in Irish and lectures on Irish religious literature, and published an Irish hymnal. Its proceedings were for a time placid, but political pressures led to a schism. In June 1916, at the annual general meeting, the members passed a resolution deploring the rising and affirming their loyalty to the king. In the following year the president and the three vice-presidents (the bishops of Tuam, Killaloe and Limerick and the dean of St Patrick's) wrote to the committee, stating they had reasons to believe that the policy of the guild was becoming that of the extreme republican party in Ireland, and asking for an assurance that the committee would abide by the resolution of June 1916. When in 1918 at the annual meeting the resolution was rescinded, the president and vice-presidents resigned, and formed a new society, Comhluadar Gaodhalach na Fiadhnuise. The Cumann Gaodhalach na h-Eaglaise continued with a reduced membership and in 1920 expressed regret that the church, through its leaders and representative laymen, was constantly identified with the reactionary forces in this country.[10]

The nationalists, political and cultural, who were members of the Church of Ireland were energetic and outspoken, but they formed a very small minority, and when the final phase of the home rule struggle began in 1912 it was abundantly clear that the Church of Ireland as a body wanted no change in the constitutional relationship between Great Britain and Ireland. A few days after Asquith moved the first reading of the third home rule bill, a special meeting of the general synod passed a resolution affirming 'unswerving attachment to the legislative union now subsisting between Great Britain and Ireland'. Hannay protested against the church committing itself on the issue, but the size of the minority against the resolution (it numbered only five) served to demonstrate the strength of unionist feeling in the general synod.

Though the members of the Church of Ireland were almost unanimous in their determination to resist home rule, they, and Irish unionists in general, became divided over one important issue – what should be their policy if the time came when home rule seemed inevitable. Then, the northern unionists were prepared to accept a compromise – the exemption from the operation of the home rule act of the north-east six counties, large community. The southern unionists naturally did not want to find themselves a small scattered minority in a divided Ireland. So, if home rule could not be defeated, their aims were to preserve the unity of Ireland with safeguards for the unionist minority. Political divergencies amongst Irish episcopalians were illustrated by the reactions of the bench towards the end of 1912 to 'Ulster Day'. The Ulster unionists had planned a great series of demonstrations which were to culminate in the signing of a covenant against home rule on 28 September. D'Arcy, the bishop of Down, without consulting the other Ulster bishops, announced that there would be special services in the churches of his diocese on the morning of the 28th. The primate and the other Ulster bishops, 'much put out by Down's action', agreed that on the previous Sunday, 22nd, there should be 'prayers on the whole matter of home rule', thus, they hoped, avoiding identifying the church with the proceedings on the 28th. Peacocke, the archbishop of Dublin, was very much afraid that if the members of the Church of Ireland were associated with the decisions of the Belfast meeting, the Hibernians and the Land League might 'raise hostility against them throughout the other provinces'. And the bishop of Cork thought that the great majority of the laity in the south 'object to being in any way identified with the Ulster movement'. Bernard, the dean of St Patrick's, suggested a compromise – that there should be special prayers on the Sunday before parliament met – and this course was agreed to by the bishops of the southern province, with at first one exception, the bishop of Cashel, O'Hara, who had been dean of Belfast. He wanted special prayers on 22 September, the day fixed by the northern bishops, but in the end Peacocke was able to tell Bernard that O'Hara 'has come round'.[11] If the southern bishops were cautious, the five bishops whose diocese covered Ulster made their position clear by signing the 1912 covenant, and a future bishop of Down, by adding the names of two retired bishops who signed (Stack of Clogher and Montgomery of Tasmania), was able to point out that, as in 1688, seven bishops had banded themselves together at a time of crisis.[12]

During 1913, while the home rule debate continued with growing acerbity, Dublin was seriously disturbed by a series of labour disputes. These do not seem to have attracted much attention in the Church of Ireland outside the Dublin diocese.

The Dublin diocesan synod called for a viceregal commission of inquiry into the conditions of housing of the poor in the city of Dublin, and towards the end of the year both the archbishop of Dublin and the dean of St Patrick's attended a meeting organized by the Dublin citizens' peace committee – in the words of the lord mayor, a meeting of 'non-combatants'. The archbishop heartily agreed that an effort should be made to bring employers and employees together, and the dean declared that, if this was done, 'their differences would disappear in half an hour'. Another Dublin clergyman, the Rev. R. M. Gwynn, a fellow of Trinity deeply interested in social questions, was present at a committee meeting (which may have been held in his college rooms) at which the formation of the citizens' army was proposed. This body was to play an important part in the 1916 rising, but Gwynn made it clear that in his opinion 'the title army was not intended to suggest military action but merely drill on military lines to keep unemployed men fit and self-respecting'.[13]

In the summer of 1914 the outbreak of the great European war for a time turned men's minds from domestic issues. Ireland, though engaged in the war, suffered relatively little, escaping devastation, severe rationing, conscription and air raids. Irish social life was not seriously dislocated, agricultural prices were high, the industries of the Belfast zone were stimulated by large and urgent wartime orders. Nevertheless, thinking men were bound to be shaken and saddened by the rapid spread of the conflict, the destruction, the suffering inflicted on non-combatants, the ever-lengthening casualty lists. The belief in human progress, political and moral, which had developed during the past century, an era of unprecedented scientific and economic advance marked by long periods of peace between the great powers, was harshly challenged. But though the war years were a time of uncertainty and pain, in one respect at least Irish churchmen were sure of their ground. They were convinced that the United Kingdom and its allies were fighting in a righteous cause – the cause of freedom and civilization against unscrupulous aggression. When the general synod met for its first wartime session, the archbishop of Armagh, Crozier, in a powerful address, declared, 'this world-wide war has been forced on us by well calculated greed and hate ... a great nation, lost to all sense of honour and decency, has exceeded the ferocity of naked savages by rapine and rape, butchery and brutality'. Christ, the primate went on to explain, had taught us we must forgive our enemies, but the German emperor and his evil vassals were not their personal enemies, they were the enemies of civilization. And, when in 1915 during a debate in the general synod on the revision of the hymnal, it was proposed that the second verse of the national anthem be omitted, one dean described it as 'a verse of strong, vigorous language, just the verse that at the present junction they all felt to be appropriate', and another dean declared that when he 'heard of the submarine dodges of Admiral Tirpitz, he prayed with all his heart that his knavish tricks might be frustrated'.

At the end of the first month of the war, the primate issued an appeal for recruits, in which he stressed that[14]

from all seeming ill God will work out good. The trivialities of life will be seen in their due perspective, the great realities of life, the things that matter will stand out in bold relief. As it was after the great Napoleonic wars of a hundred years ago, so it would be again in the year of grace 1915. Literature will be revived as it was by Sir Walter Scott and his contemporaries. Religion will become a great factor in human life, and the breaking up of German aggressive militarism will bring a long and lasting peace.

Irish churchmen shared in the primate's belief that the empire was fighting a just war, and the war memorials in Church of Ireland churches, with their long list of names, are a sobering reminder of the costly contribution which members of the church made to the war effort. It is difficult to state precisely the size of that contribution, but statistics are available which are a help towards measuring it. At the close of the first year of the war, according to diocesan estimates, the proportion of the Church of Ireland population serving with the forces was in the diocese of Down 5 per cent, in Dublin 6 per cent, in Cashel 6·5 per cent, in Ossory one in thirty; in Ferns one in thirty-one.[15] A year later, rather more than two years after the outbreak of the war, the official figures were released which indicated that about 21,000 members of the Church of Ireland had joined the forces. It is perhaps worth noting that this official return shows that the response varied somewhat between the different provinces. In Ulster one protestant in twenty-two had joined the forces, in Leinster one in thirty-six, in Connaught one in sixty-three.[16] An explanation for this is provided by an official report on recruiting in Ireland. Referring to the agricultural areas in Ireland, it pointed out that it was difficult to 'make an impression on a scattered population of conservative tendencies' at a time when of course farming could be held to be an important public service. Recruiting in the Church of Ireland community was undoubtedly influenced by this factor. But, as has been seen, the response was on the whole impressive, and represented a severe drain on a small church. It was bound, too, to have an especially noticeable impact on parishes with a scanty and scattered Church of Ireland population. Such parishes were bound to suffer not only from the losses in the field, but from the fact that recruiting, by uprooting young men at a critical stage in their life, accelerated the impulse to emigrate.

During the war years, members of the Church of Ireland were not only deeply concerned about the progress of the war, they were also profoundly disturbed by political developments in Ireland. At the beginning of the war it seemed as if at last almost the whole of Ireland was united in a common cause. But a small section of the more extreme nationalists urged that Ireland should not support the British war effort and in 1916 some of their leaders decided on direct action against British authority in Ireland. On Easter Monday a number of buildings were seized in Dublin by the Irish volunteers and the citizen army, and an Irish republic was proclaimed. The rising was suppressed by the crown forces after a week of strenuous street fighting, but from then on the more extreme nationalist movement, usually called Sinn Fein, which aimed at complete independence, steadily gained support in nationalist Ireland.

During the Easter Rising in Dublin a number of the Church of Ireland clergy showed themselves 'fearless of danger' as they went among the poor, visited hospitals and helped the wounded under fire.[17] The bishop of Tuam, the Honourable Benjamin Plunket, had an alarming experience. His car was seized in St Stephen's Green and used to make a barricade. 'Realizing things were serious,' the bishop 'gave his card to a Sinn Feiner', and his car was immediately returned to him.[18] The archbishop of Dublin, Bernard, was in the thick of the battle, his palace overlooking St Stephen's Green where the insurgents were entrenched. Bernard's reaction to the rebellion was what might have been predicted. He was a convinced unionist, who, it was said, could not conceive 'of any stronger sanction than the duty of obedience to the existing order'. Early in May in a short letter to *The Times* he emphasized that martial law was then the only security for life and property in Dublin, adding 'this is not the time for amnesties and pardons, it is the time for punishment swift and stern'. A month later he told Lloyd George, that 'the Irish people have been taught that crime – small or great – may expect to escape punishment if only it can assume a political complexion. . . . The tradition of yielding to sentimental clamour when law breakers are to be punished is a *damnosa hereditas*.'[19]

Bernard was profoundly conscious of the value of law and order. In 1918 he pointed out to a country clergyman who had publicly avowed himself an opponent of conscription that, though he had the right to protest against conscription, if he associated with those who resisted the law he would 'bring dishonour on the Church of Ireland in this province, which has always upheld the tradition of obedience to the law, as a Christian duty, recommended in the New Testament'.[20] But Bernard was not politically inflexible. At the close of 1916 he was vigorously impressing on unionists that the home rule act of 1914 was a political fact which they could not ignore, and he strove for an Irish settlement which would give Ireland a measure of autonomy, sufficient, in Bernard's opinion, to satisfy reasonable nationalists while maintaining the unity of Ireland and preserving many links with Great Britain. Bernard failed and though he was undoubtedly the greatest ecclesiastical statesman in the Church of Ireland – perhaps in Ireland – he failed to preserve the unity of even the episcopal bench. In May 1917 three Church of Ireland bishops, Tuam, Ossory and Killaloe, together with seventeen Roman catholic bishops, signed a declaration against partition. Immediately afterwards the primate and the four Ulster bishops issued a declaration pointing out that the Church of Ireland had not receded from the opinion it thrice expressed that home rule would be 'disastrous to the best interests of Ireland and dangerous to the empire', adding that no scheme of home rule could be carried 'without the exclusion of Ulster'.[21]

The failure of the moderate nationalists and the unionists to

arrive at an agreed settlement was to have catastrophic consequences for the Church of Ireland in the south and west. In
January 1919 the Sinn Fein MPs elected to Westminster at the
general election at the end of 1918 met in Dublin and declared
Ireland to be an independent republic, and for three years
passive and active methods were employed to undermine the
authority of the crown in Ireland. Soon the police, harassed by
attacks, were withdrawn from many outlying stations, the
courts practically speaking ceased to function and guerrilla
warfare – including inevitably acts of terrorism and reprisals –
spread over much of the countryside and broke out in cities and
towns. The struggle of the republican army against the crown
forces ended in July 1921, but less than a year later the civil war
between the pro- and anti-treaty parties began which led to some
fighting and a considerable amount of economic dislocation in the
south and west. It was not until 1923 that Ireland was at peace.

Members of the Church of Ireland in the three southern
provinces were badly shaken by the breakdown of the conventional machinery for the maintenance of law and order.
Furthermore, the premises on which the more extreme nationalists justified their actions placed them in a difficult and dangerous situation. It was argued that Dail Eireann and its agents
formed the legitimate government of Ireland and possessed the
right to command the obedience and support of all Irishmen
in the struggle against the aggressive invasion being conducted
by the crown forces. To members of the Church of Ireland,
attached for generations to the existing regime and imbued
with an intense loyalty to the crown, the republican argument
must have seemed immoral if not simply fantastic. Nevertheless,
it meant that two absolutes were in conflict, and an Irish
unionist who continued (in his own opinion) as a loyal subject
and a good citizen to support law and order in the face of
outrage might find himself regarded by some of his neighbours
as a traitor to the community and an ally of alien and oppressive
force. Certainly there was no declared hostility to protestants
on religious grounds. But the protestant was often a unionist in
areas where a unionist was a *rara avis*. In the spring of 1922, after
a number of protestants in the south had been compelled by
threats to leave their homes and some in county Cork had been
murdered, the members of the general synod resident in the

twenty-six counties appointed a deputation to interview the provisional government. The deputation, on being received by General Michael Collins and William Cosgrave, asked if the government was 'desirous of retaining' the protestant community in the country. It was assured that the government would take every step in its power to protect all citizens of the state, and that 'the Belfast massacres could not be regarded as any justification for the outrages'.[22] Of course it must be also taken into account that during the disturbed years 1919–23, over most of Ireland for most of the time life continued on normal or almost normal lines and there were wide areas in which little untoward ever happened. Moreover, many members of the Church of Ireland remained on good terms with their neighbours – after all, men had other interests as well as politics and in the worst circumstances good nature could break through. Still, many members of the Church of Ireland were bound to be badly shaken by the disappearance of familiar, reassuring political landmarks. 'The last year', a member of the Church of Ireland wrote to archbishop Bernard late in 1921,[23]

has made me feel for the first time that I am myself essentially English not Irish. . . . A man is what he inherits and what he draws from his surroundings and for me and for most of us protestants these things are ninety per cent English or Scotch – traditions, beliefs, customs, mental furniture, all that: and why I mainly fear and draw back from the new order, which I suppose will flood in upon us sooner or later, is not so much the material loss and annoyance as the tendency to cut us away from our roots, our civilisation which is bone of our bone, flesh of our flesh.

From 1922 the Church of Ireland was working in the two separate states between which Ireland was divided, the Irish Free State and the United Kingdom. The Irish Free State, comprising twenty-six counties and about two-thirds of the population of the island, formed a self-governing dominion within the British commonwealth until 1937, when it adopted a republican form of constitution while remaining associated with the commonwealth. In 1949 this association was terminated when the twenty-six counties became the Republic of Ireland. The six north-east counties, Northern Ireland, remained part of the United Kingdom, but enjoyed a substantial measure of home rule. They had their own government and parliament on which devolved responsibility for a number of services within the area. The great majority of the members of the Church of Ireland were, as has been said, within Northern Ireland, but the machinery of the church remained largely based in the south. Of the thirteen diocesans only five worked and three lived in Northern Ireland. The divinity school and the head-quarters of the representative church body remained in Dublin and the general synod continued to meet there. This meant that the Church of Ireland remained a unifying force in Irish life, northern churchmen interested in ecclesiastical administration being kept in touch with Dublin. It also may have nourished an archaic view of the church's position.

Relations between church and state in each area were, so far as the Church of Ireland was concerned, undramatic. For many years after 1922 change came comparatively slowly in Ireland, both north and south, and there were few issues in which religious considerations were involved which greatly exercised Church of Ireland opinion. Of course many members of the Church of Ireland accepted the regime in the south reluctantly. 'God save the King was a prayer that rose spontaneously to their lips and was the expression of their hearts' devotions',[24] but in Free State political life even the supporters of the treaty tended to minimize the significance of the crown and the commonwealth association. The attitude of the Church of Ireland was reflected in the changes made in the state prayers. The changes made in 1926 were minimal, being simply an insertion of petitions for the governors and parliaments in Northern Ireland and the Irish Free State (the southern legisla-ture which officially, even in the English language, was always referred to by its Gaelic name, being firmly termed a parliament in the prayer book). In 1939 it was decided that no changes should be made in the state prayers, though the house of bishops was empowered to permit such alterations 'as they may deem necessary to fit them to the then present circumstances'. The twenty-six counties were still in an unsentimental and un-stressed fashion connected with the British commonwealth, so the Church of Ireland attitude, though fundamentally it represented a clinging to old loyalties, could on constitutional grounds be justified. But in 1949, after the twenty-six counties had become the Republic of Ireland, the state prayers to be used were amended to conform to the republican form of government. 'Many dwellers in the Republic', archbishop Gregg declared at this time, 'will regret the loss of the familiar words but what other way is there? . . . For in our prayers above all, there must be reality.'

There were two social issues on which the Irish Free State shortly after its foundation declared its firm adherence to the teachings of the Roman catholic church – divorce and birth control. From 1870 the probate and matrimonial division of the high court in Ireland had power to grant a divorce *a mensa et thoro* (a judicial separation); but a suitor domiciled in Ireland who desired the dissolution of his marriage had to obtain a private act of parliament. In 1925 the oireachtas, when discussing standing orders relating to private bills, made it clear that it was determined to prevent divorces *a vinculo matrimonii* being granted in the state, and the constitution of 1937 provided that 'no law shall be enacted providing for the grant of a dissolution of marriage'. 'The whole fabric of our social organization', President Cosgrave explained in 1925, 'is based upon the sanctity of the marriage bond and anything that tends to weaken that bond to that extent strikes at the root of our social life.'[25]

The official anglican attitude to the problem was expressed by the Lambeth conferences of 1920 and 1930. The conference of 1920 declared that marriage was a lifelong and indissoluble union, though taking into account Matt. 19:3–9 it thought that a man might be permitted to divorce an unfaithful spouse. The conference of 1930 recommended that 'the marriage of one whose former partner is still living should not be celebrated according to the rites of the church'. Early in 1925, shortly after the divorce question had been discussed in the dail, the archbishop of Dublin in an impressive sermon emphasized that the anglican church had 'always fought unflinchingly for the indissolubility of marriage', adding, however, that individuals here and there undoubtedly felt aggrieved by being shut out by legislation from relief which Our Lord seems to have contemplated. Some months later the bishop of Meath, in an address to the mothers' union, declared that if divorce was to be granted it should only be 'for the one reason laid down by Christ', that the guilty party should not under any circumstances be allowed to marry again and should be treated not only as a sinner but as a criminal.[26] This address was sharply censured by W. B. Yeats, who in the course of an impassionate attack on the Roman catholic attitude to divorce delivered in the senate, said that 'it was one of the glories of the church in which I was born that we have put our bishops in their places in discussions requiring legislation'. In the oireachtas debates of 1925 two leading laymen, Bagwell in the senate and Thrift, later provost of Trinity, in the dail, while stressing their own dislike of divorce, argued that it was wrong to impose the religious view of the majority on members of the minority. However another member of the oireachtas who belonged to 'the late established church' was strongly against granting facilities for divorce.[27]

The censorship act of 1929 forbade the sale or distribution of books or periodicals 'advocating the unnatural prevention of conception', and when the act was greatly amended in 1946 this prohibition was continued. The Lambeth conference of 1920 had uttered an emphatic warning against the use of unnatural means for the avoidance of conception, but anglican opinion on the question was changing and in 1930, to the dismay of high churchmen such as Gore, the conference declared that other methods than 'complete abstinence from intercourse may be used to limit or avoid parenthood'. Obviously then there was a growing divergency between the churches on the subject of birth control, and in the debates on the censorship bill, leading Church of Ireland laymen criticized the provision relating to literature advocating birth control. Thrift found it difficult to 'lay down a hard and fast line'. Though he was aware that the indiscriminate circulation of birth-control literature 'was undoubtedly leading to the spread of sexual immorality because it indicated that sexual immorality could take place without the natural consequences', he nevertheless was against the automatic banning of all writings on the subject. In the senate, Sir John Keane, a man of strong and independent intellect, reminded his hearers that there were 'certain people who are fully Christian, who are fully high minded and who have a sense of social duty who do claim that there are cases where the use of contraceptives is legitimate', and Bagwell, having pointed out that 'there were innumerable examples in the world of what was once anathema becoming accepted fact', suggested this might occur in the instance of that 'contentious question' birth control.[28]

Twenty years later a third issue disturbed the members of the Church of Ireland living in the Republic. In 1950 the supreme court set aside the prevailing rule that a father had a right to break an ante-nuptial agreement made by the parties to a marriage dealing with questions which might arise during the marriage (including the education of children). It was argued that the 'paternal prepotency' established by the old rule was alien to modern views on the equality of the sexes, that there was 'no injustice in holding a man to his pledge' and that the new decision was more in accordance with public policy than the rule.[29] But the minority could not help noticing that the change in the rule favoured the Roman catholic party in the 1950 case, and furthermore that the Roman catholic church, with its strict rules on 'mixed marriages', was the religious body which stood to gain from the enforcement of ante-nuptial pledges.

One question, education, which in the past had been a subject of vehement debate, aroused surprisingly little controversy. The educational system in the south remained for forty years after the establishment of the Irish Free State remarkably unchanged in general outline, with primary education completely, and secondary education to a very great extent, under the control of the churches. The Church of Ireland was, however, confronted with two problems – the education in their own religious environment of children belonging to isolated Church of Ireland families and the place of Irish in the educational system. In 1932 it was estimated that there were in the Irish Free State, 1,300 protestant children outside reasonable walking distance of a school under protestant control. Determined efforts were made by the church to provide them with transport to the nearest protestant school, lengthy negotiations being conducted with the department of education. Diocesan schemes were devised, local funds raised, the representative church body made an annual grant and the government agreed to make a substantial contribution. The result was satisfactory and even during the early 1940s 'in spite of shortage of petrol, rubber, batteries, etc.' the bus services were maintained.[30]

The place of Irish in primary education was not settled so easily. Many Irish nationalists fervently believed that independence would be culturally meaningful only if the citizens of the state could express themselves through the language which in the distant past had been spoken throughout Ireland. It was the declared intention of the new regime 'to work with all its might for the strengthening of the national fibre by giving the language, history, music, and tradition of Ireland their natural place in the life of Irish schools'.[31] This meant that in the primary schools Irish became a compulsory subject and that as far as possible other subjects were to be taught through the medium of Irish. It was pointed out by the department of education that 'in the movement that has done so much for the national revival in Irish education representatives of the minority have been amongst the pioneers and the most serious workers'. This was no doubt true and, indeed, on one occasion the Church of Ireland board of education itself pointed out that 'the modern Gaelic movement could with some accuracy be described as the child of a Church of Ireland man – Douglas Hyde',[32] but the Church of Ireland in general showed little interest in the Irish revival. This is scarcely surprising. As the Church of Ireland board of education also pointed out, 'English is the home language of most of our families as it is the language of the Bible, the prayer book and the church formularies', and most members of the Church of Ireland had political loyalties which were bound to compete with, or even run counter to, the forces which encouraged and were inspired by the Gaelic revival.

From the beginning of the new regime, the Church of Ireland board of education was critical of the government's Irish policy. At the outset, in 1923, the board complained that the Irish phrase books for primary schools contained 'some – many of them too much – Roman catholic doctrine' and that 'the books by P. Pearse' on the teachers' training course were open to grave objections. The minister of education replied that if equivalent books to those said to be unsuitable for protestant schools were suggested he would see they were substituted. In 1926 the board expressed its regret that Irish was a compulsory subject, pointing out that owing to the amount of time which had to be devoted to it, certain desirable subjects had to be excluded from the curriculum, and ten years later the board declared itself opposed to teaching children in a language other than that spoken at home. But when in 1938 Sir John Keane proposed a motion in the general synod to the effect that the synod should request the government to carry out an independent inquiry into teaching through the medium of Irish, caution prevailed. It was decided to pass on to the next business, it being argued that 'if they mentioned the subject of Irish they might be quite misunderstood'. But in 1939 the board of education issued a strong statement on the use of Irish in primary schools. The curriculum, it declared, had to be restricted and 'except in schools where the teacher and pupils alike are of supernormal capacity the development of the pupils has been retarded'. Ninety-nine per cent of the Church of Ireland managers, it added, were opposed to compulsory teaching through Irish. Ten years later, in 1949, the board returned to the attack. In a long memorandum on primary education, which it submitted to the minister, it emphasized that children should be taught through the medium of Irish only if it was their mother tongue. 'Not to use the home language of the children', the board stated, 'be it Irish or English is a psychological outrage upon the most helpless and inarticulate section of the community.' Some years later, in a memorandum on secondary education, the board declared that a failure in Irish should not entail failure in an entire examination. The cause of the Irish language, it argued, 'would be better served by a system of incentives, and scholarships rather than by one of attempted compulsion'. And two years later it boldly declared that if compulsory Irish was abolished in the schools of the Republic, 'the sense of nationality would still keep up enthusiasm for the subject in the protestant schools of the Republic'.

Strangely enough it was in Northern Ireland that there occurred the most striking clash between the Church of Ireland and the state over an educational issue. From the time it was constituted, the government of Northern Ireland devoted considerable attention to educational problems, and two major measures, the education acts of 1923 and 1947, made far-reaching changes. The government (or the ministry of education) was eager to raise standards and streamline the educational system, and seems to have regarded denominationalism as a hindrance to educational progress. The ministry was dismayed by the number of primary schools with muddy playgrounds or no playgrounds at all, badly heated rooms, antiquated and unsuitable furniture, equipment limited to the barest necessities and sanitary accommodation crude, unhealthy and inadequate. The managers of these schools, 'almost without exception persons of culture and humane dispositions', must, the ministry felt, share its dismay at the condition of their schools. The 1923 act created local educational authorities and laid down that there should be three types of primary school, provided, transferred and voluntary, a provided school being a school founded by the local education authority, a transferred school being a school handed over by the manager to the local education authority. Though the church lost control over the schools transferred, guarantees against secularization were provided and, in the event, a number of Church of Ireland schools were transferred. By 1945 over three-quarters of the Church of Ireland primary school children were attending provided or transferred schools though there were still about 150 primary schools under Church of Ireland control.

The 1947 act effected revolutionary changes in the educational system. Its main principle was that 'all children should be educated according to their differing ages, abilities and aptitude, primary and secondary education being regarded as progressive stages'. This implied not only considerable improvements in the facilities for primary education, but the provision of grammar and secondary schools and technical colleges. In all schools there was to be religious instruction, and arrangements were to be made in schools under a local education authority for denominational instruction of children whose parents desired it. The Northern Ireland committee of the board of education welcomed the bill in general, but expressed great concern over one important issue – the position of teachers. Both the board and the government agreed that there should be a 'conscience clause' for teachers, so that no teacher could be compelled to give religious instruction. But the committee wanted the appointing bodies – on which the transferors of primary schools would be represented – to be able to inquire into a teacher's beliefs when making an appointment and a vigorous attempt was made to get the bill amended. Deputations interviewed the prime minister and the minister of education and in November 1946, at a large meeting in Belfast, it was suggested that a fighting fund of £20,000 should be raised. At this meeting a letter was read from the primate, Dr Gregg, which declared that the government was breaking faith with the transferors, that there must be sufficient protestant teachers to teach protestant children and that country schools must not be deprived of children who had reached the age of eleven. The government refused to yield and the Northern Ireland committee of the board, convinced that the act 'opens up the way to the complete secularisation of the teaching profession', seems to have contemplated ceasing to transfer Church of Ireland schools or even reversing the process. But church opinion was divided. At the general synod of 1947 the bishops of Down and Connor made it clear they did not support the Northern Ireland committee of the board. The transfer of Church of Ireland schools continued and, at the beginning of the 1960s, it was decided that the primary schools remaining under the control of the Church of Ireland should be transferred 'in order to preserve as many transferors' rights as possible'.

Despite the differences in educational and social policy, there were times when the Church of Ireland could almost forget that it was working in two distinct states. But this was certainly not so between 1939 and 1945. During these years Northern Ireland, as part of the United Kingdom, was at war while the south, 'Eire' as it was generally termed, remained neutral. In many Northern Ireland parishes much energy was poured into branches of welfare work especially required in wartime circumstances, and the church in Belfast suffered severely in the air-raids on the city in 1941, four churches being destroyed and twelve others damaged. Many members of the Church of Ireland from both north and south served in the forces, and the attitude of the church as a whole was reflected in the addresses given by the primate, Dr Gregg, at the opening of the general synod. In May 1940 archbishop Gregg explained that, though some might have expected him to make 'an extended reference' to the war, 'I do not propose to take advantage of the hospitality of the neutral country, within whose borders we are assembled to do so'. But in 1941 he spoke of how their hearts were filled with thankful wonder that the forces of the empire still held their own, and in 1943 he declared that 'the cause of the allied nations is the cause of freedom and justice'.

VI

THE CHURCH IN THE
TWENTIETH CENTURY

~~~~~~

THE YEAR 1911 was a point at which Irish churchmen might well pause and take stock of their position. It was just forty years from disestablishment and it was a census year. Moreover, though no one could have realized it, Irishmen were at the end of an era of relative political tranquillity and on the threshold of an age which was to be marked by political crises, war and civil strife. The 1911 census showed that the population of Ireland was still declining, having fallen from 5,412,000 in 1871 to 4,390,000 in 1911. During this period the Church of Ireland population had also fallen – from 667,900 to 576,600. Thus, relatively speaking, the Church of Ireland had retained its position, indeed it was fractionally stronger. In 1871 the members of the Church of Ireland had amounted to 12·34 per cent of the population, in 1911 they were 13·13 per cent. These figures might convey a mistaken impression of stability, but in fact in some areas there had been significant changes in the denominational balance, and the distribution of the Church of Ireland population in Ireland as a whole had altered considerably. The Church of Ireland population in Connaught had fallen from 36,000 to 19,000; from 4·2 per cent of the population to 3·1. This decline can be partly accounted for by the fact that in 1911 there were 1,000 fewer protestant soldiers and policemen in the province than in 1871. But it is also noticeable that the number of protestant farmers had fallen by almost one-third – from 2,887 to 2,089, and protestant farm workers, who in 1871 had numbered only 1,957, by 1911 amounted to fewer than 350. In the three western counties of Munster – Clare, Kerry and Limerick (including Limerick city) – the trend was the same as in Connaught. Between 1871 and 1911 the Church of Ireland population fell from 17,000 to 10,300 and from 2·9 per cent of the total population of the three counties to 2·3 per cent. The Church of Ireland population had also fallen steeply in the two principal Munster urban centres, Cork and Waterford. In Cork in 1911 it was down to forming only 8·6 per cent of the population, having been 11·7 per cent in 1871. But taking Munster as a whole, the outlook for the Church of Ireland was somewhat more cheerful. In Tipperary its relative position had declined only slightly, from forming 5·1 of the population in 1871 to being 4·74 in 1911. And in two counties, Cork and Waterford, it had relatively improved its position since 1871 – in Cork, from forming 7·1 per cent of the population to forming 7·29; in Waterford from forming 2·9 per cent to forming 3·59. In Munster between 1871 and 1911 the membership of the Church of Ireland dropped from 74,000 to 50,650 but, relatively speaking, it almost held its own; in 1871 its membership amounted to 5·3 per cent of the population of the province, in 1911 to 4·89 per cent.

In Leinster the Church of Ireland relatively held its position between 1871 and 1911, though its membership declined from 164,000 to 140,000. In 1871 it formed 12·3 per cent of the population, in 1911 12·1 per cent. Of its membership in Leinster, well over half (78,000) was in the city and county of Dublin and its numbers in this zone had remained stationary. But as it was one of the few areas in Ireland with an increasing population, the Church of Ireland percentage of the population had fallen from 19·5 to 16·5. Directly to the south of county Dublin in county Wicklow, the Church of Ireland, though it had declined in numbers, had relatively improved its position since 1871, its percentage of the population having risen from 17·7 to 18·4. To the west of county Dublin, in county Kildare, the Church of Ireland membership had increased both relatively (from 12 per cent in 1871 to 15·8 per cent) and absolutely. But this can be explained by a rise of 1,100 episcopalians in the army. In all the other Leinster counties there was an absolute and relative decline in the Church of Ireland membership. But if the trend was downwards, it was not conspicuous enough to be alarming.

In Ulster between 1871 and 1911 the Church of Ireland population had fallen only slightly, from 393,000 to 366,700, and proportionately speaking it had increased from being 20·4 per cent of the population of the province to being 23·1 per cent. In all the Ulster counties the Church of Ireland population had numerically declined. In three, Down, Londonderry and Tyrone, it had relatively increased, in six it had relatively declined. In the south and west of Ulster – the counties of Donegal, Fermanagh, Monaghan and Cavan – the Church of Ireland population fell from 109,000 to 60,800 and its percentage of the total population of these counties declined from 21 to 15. But the most striking change in Ulster was the growth of Belfast. Between 1871 and 1911 the Church of Ireland population of the city almost trebled, rising from 46,000 to 118,000. Relatively, too, the Church of Ireland improved its position in the city. In 1871 it comprised 26·6 per cent of the population, in 1911 30·5. In fact, by 1911 over a quarter of the total membership of the Church of Ireland lived in Belfast and over 40 per cent lived in the north-east area – Belfast and the counties of Antrim, Armagh and Down. If Belfast and the six counties which constitute Northern Ireland are taken together, their inhabitants included 56 per cent of the members of the Church of Ireland (compared with just under 50 in 1871).

Turning to occupational statistics, during the forty years that elapsed from disestablishment, the Church of Ireland had lost its commanding position in the professional world, though it still possessed more than its proportionate share of the professions, with almost 34 per cent of the clergy, over 37 per cent of the barristers and solicitors, 26 per cent of the law clerks, almost 30 per cent of the doctors and dentists, and just over 40 per cent of civil engineers. Four-fifths of the army officers resident in Ireland and just over 60 per cent of the rank and file serving there were episcopalians. But the Church of Ireland share in the police (just over 16 per cent) and in the civil service (just under 25 per cent) had fallen since 1871. In the business world the Church of Ireland was losing ground, though it was still strong with 13·6 per cent of the merchants, nearly 42 per cent of those engaged in banking, just under 26 per cent of the accountants, 25 per cent of commercial travellers, over 24 per cent of commercial clerks and 31 per cent of the brokers and auctioneers. In the retail trades the Church of Ireland was slightly stronger than in 1871, with 13 per cent of the grocers, just over 10 per cent of the poulterers, just over 9 per cent of the butchers and greengrocers, just under 9 per cent of the 'shop-keepers', and only 4 per cent of fishmongers (perhaps it should be added that the Church of Ireland had a much stronger position in the retail trades in Ulster than in Ireland in general but, even so, weaker than its numbers demanded). In one important sphere the Church of Ireland was definitely weaker – there had been a considerable fall in the number of Church of Ireland farmers. In 1871 they numbered 42,000, by 1911 they amounted to only 29,300. The total number of farmers in Ireland had in fact fallen, but the church loss was disproportionately great, so that by 1911 only 7·6 per cent of Irish farmers were members of the Church of Ireland. The number of Church of Ireland farm labourers fell even more drastically, from 26,000 in 1871 to 15,000 in 1911. And while in 1871 there had been 6,000 Church of Ireland farm labourers in the three southern provinces, in 1911 there were only 1,500, about 90 per cent of the total being in Ulster. There was another feature of the census returns which had somewhat ominous implications. Though the members of the Church of Ireland amounted to 13·13 per cent of the population, they were only 12·3 of those undergoing instruction at school and college. In Ulster indeed, where episcopalians were 23·19 per cent of the total population, they were 23·8 per cent of those receiving instruction. So it seemed probable that in some parts of Ireland the Church of Ireland, from the age distribution of its membership, would shrink proportionately to the remainder of the population.

If during the forty years following disestablishment the Church of Ireland population pattern remained remarkably consistent, the decades following the First World War witnessed striking changes. In the three southern provinces the picture presented by the census returns is grim. Between 1911 and 1926 the membership of the Church of Ireland in the twenty-six counties fell from 250,000 to 164,000, a decline in fifteen years of 34 per cent. The census report for 1926 suggests that the withdrawal of the police, army and navy with their dependants accounted for 25,000 of the loss. To this must be added war casualties, and there was in this period a 5 per cent decline in the population of the twenty-six counties. But even if these facts are allowed for, the rate of emigration, presumably largely owing to political reasons, must have been very high. The catastrophic fall in numbers between 1911 and 1926 was followed by a steady decline, and by 1961 the Church of Ireland population in the twenty-six counties which formed the Republic of Ireland had fallen to 104,000 (a fall of 36 per cent in thirty-five years) and it amounted to only 3·7 per cent of the total population of the Republic. In the Dublin area (city and county) the Church of Ireland was comparatively strong, having 38,000 members, 5·3 per cent of the total population of the area and nearly 60 per cent of all the members of the Church of Ireland in Leinster. In Connaught there were under 7,000 members of the Church of Ireland. In Cavan and Monaghan there were 7,900 episcopalians (7·6 per cent of the total population of the two counties). In Donegal there were 7,345 episcopalians (6·4 per cent of the population of the county).

There are some obvious explanations for this fall in numbers. In the second quarter of the century the birth rate among episcopalians was slightly under that of the twenty-six counties as a whole and their emigration rate was high. It has been calculated that one-third of the protestant males in the twenty-six counties who came of age during the early 1940s emigrated (compared with one-quarter of the Roman catholic males in the same category). Finally, over wide areas the Church of Ireland was bound to suffer the erosion which usually weakens a small, scattered community, not sharply separated from its neighbours by linguistic differences or perceptible racial characteristics. The occupation distribution of the Church of Ireland population of the twenty-six counties in 1961 reflected in a diminished and declining form its historic social status. Of farmers whose holdings were under thirty acres, only 2·3 per cent were members of the Church of Ireland; but almost 20 per cent of the farmers with holdings of over 200 acres were members of that church. Only 9·8 per cent of labourers and unskilled workers were members of the Church of Ireland; but the church's membership included 8·7 per cent of clerks, about 8 per cent of medical doctors, almost 11 per cent of engineers and architects and 20 per cent of company directors, managers and company secretaries.

In Northern Ireland, where, from the seventeenth century, there had been large episcopalian communities, the statistical position was much more cheerful. In 1911 and 1926 the membership of the Church of Ireland in the area rose slightly and it made a small proportionate gain (from being 26 per cent to being 27 per cent of the population). Then between 1926 and 1961 there was a further small increase in numbers from 338,000 to 344,000 (though there was a comparative loss, the episcopalians sinking to being 24 per cent of the total population). Taking Northern Ireland and the Republic together, in 1961 there were 449,000 members of the Church of Ireland in Ireland, forming 10·5 per cent of the total population. Three-quarters of the church's membership was by then in Northern Ireland, and just over half (52 per cent) of the episcopalians in Ireland lived in two counties, Antrim and Down (including the county borough of Belfast, in which one-quarter of the members of the Church of Ireland were to be found).

The population changes which occurred after the beginning of the twentieth century demanded a redistribution of the church's resources, especially in clerical manpower. This demand was imperatively reinforced after 1914 by economic pressure, the war accentuating tendencies which had been developing for some years. In the summer of 1914 three bishops, when addressing their diocesan synods, had referred to a decline in the number of ordination candidates, and one of them, O'Hara of Cashel, bluntly stated that this was because existing clerical stipends often 'scarcely provided a living wage', and that the cost of living was increasing.[1] During the war it swept upwards fast. Many of the clergy living on fixed incomes obviously found it hard to make ends meet and some dismal clerical budgets were published. One rector stated that on 'a nominal £200 per annum he had to manage a rectory of "huge dimensions" and a maid and a man'. Another declared that his net income (including £70 per annum from grazing and produce of glebe and garden, and deducting the wages of a maid and a man and the cost of keeping a pony and trap) amounted to only £121 per annum. And it was even said that there were clergymen and their families who would be thankful for gifts of cast-off clothes.[2]

Probably the more extreme instances of clerical poverty tended to be stressed, but nevertheless it was quite clear that, at a time of rapid inflation, clerical incomes required to be readjusted, and any consideration of clerical incomes naturally led to some attention being paid to the distribution of clerical manpower. About the close of 1916, church reform began to be widely discussed. In December 1916 the representative church body appointed a committee to inquire into the union of parishes in thinly populated districts. Early in 1917 the bishop of Killaloe preached a powerful sermon in which he urged that parochial and diocesan monies should, as far as possible, be thrown into a common pool, that steps be taken to prevent an incumbent being tied too long to the same parish, that there should be a 'clergy redistribution scheme', and that where amalgamations created a parish covering a very wide area, more use should be made of 'earnest and faithful laymen' in conducting church services.[3] In March an influential conference of lay and clerical delegates nominated by diocesan clerical societies met in Dublin and expressed itself strongly in favour of the assimilation of diocesan funds and the amalgamation of parishes. Later in the year the general synod reappointed, with a greatly enlarged membership, the representative church body's committee of inquiry into the union of parishes, and in the following year, 1918, this committee reported, listing a number of parishes which should be united.

In 1919 the general synod authorized the payment of a war bonus to the clergy by the creation of a central emergency fund for the augmentation of clerical stipends. But this fund grew relatively slowly – after a year it amounted to about £10,000 – and there seems to have been a widespread feeling that the church authorities were not showing a sufficient sense of urgency. In 1920 two organizations, intent on ecclesiastical reorganization, were appealing for support, the church reform league and the clerical defence union. The aims of the church reform league were a reorganization of the church's finances, a reduction of clerical manpower, the amalgamation of parishes, and 'a readaptation of the Church's resources' to modern needs.

The clerical defence league aimed at an increase of stipends, a reduction of glebe charges, the amalgamation of parishes, an investigation of the representative church body's 'earmarked' funds and the introduction of new blood into diocesan councils, the general synod and the representative church body. What was wanted, its secretary explained, was a union of clergymen, which would, while avoiding the excesses of the trade unions, prevent the appointment of clergy to inadequately remunerated posts by informing candidates of the actual financial conditions, in vacant parishes.[4]

But just about the time the reform agitation was well under way, the representative church body confounded its critics by producing a comprehensive if moderate reform programme. In December 1919 it had appointed a small and able committee to consider retrenchment and reform, and this committee in 1920 presented the general synod with a brisk, business-like report. It began by recommending that there should be a minimum stipend of £400 for incumbents, and £200 rising to £250 for curates. At this time the average salaries for masters in protestant secondary schools ranged from £171 per annum (average for assistant masters) to £244 (average for principals).[5] In the civil service the second division clerk at his maximum with the war bonus had a salary of approximately £600 per annum. Recognizing that 'the lack of sufficient work presents a problem no less seriously acute than the insufficiency of present stipends' and that there was in many areas 'a very great waste of man power and money in maintaining an ecclesiastical establishment vastly in excess of the local requirements', the committee recommended that there should be amalgamations of parishes and adjustments of parish boundaries. Realizing the strength of 'sentiment and local influences', it further recommended that a commission should be set up empowered to carry out these changes. The committee was not in favour of a reduction in the number of bishops because the dioceses were already large, and it considered it would be difficult to consolidate the various diocesan financial schemes – the ratio of assessment to stipends differed in the various dioceses and some dioceses 'had husbanded their resources much more than others' – but it suggested the creation of a central church fund to assist in paying stipends. It also suggested that there should be superannuation arrangements which would ensure the compulsory retirement of all clergymen (including bishops) at seventy, adding that no scheme could be considered satisfactory 'which depends on voluntary retirement'. But the committee thought that a superannuated clergyman might be licensed to take charge of a parish designated as 'a light parish'.

In November 1920 a special session of the general synod was held to give legislative force to the proposals of the reform and retrenchment committee, and statutes were passed fixing the suggested minimum stipends, setting up a central church fund, establishing 'light duty parishes', and constituting a committee, appointed for five years, which was empowered to unite parishes. By this time this commission had ceased to function, some drastic changes had been made in the church's parochial structure. Between 1920 and 1926 the number of parochial clergy working in the Church of Ireland fell from 1,361 to 1,162 – a decline of 14·6 per cent – and the number of parochial units was reduced by 12·5 per cent – from 1,114 to 973. In the western dioceses – Tuam, Killaloe and Limerick – the number of incumbencies was reduced from 151 to 111 and the number of clergy working in these three dioceses fell from 179 to 122. It may be added that the amalgamation of country benefices at this time was facilitated by the advent of the motor car. In 1907 the *Church of Ireland gazette* had pointed out that the motor show 'need not look to the Irish clergy for any practical patronage' – after all it was impossible to buy a sound car for less than £120 and its maintenance would cost £50 a year. But in 1920 the Lincoln motor company took a page in the *Gazette* to advertise 'The Chevrolet – the car for the clergy'. The 'parson's progress', the advertisement declared, 'is largely a matter of locomotion.' With a car it was possible for a rector to conduct Sunday services in more than one church. A less favourable result of the advent of the motor car was mentioned as early as 1905, when the bishop of Limerick complained that government officials were seen rushing over the country in motor cars during the time of divine service.[6]

But while the number of clergy in the southern dioceses was being reduced, there was a marked increase in the number serving in Belfast – from about 65 in 1914 to about 80 in 1939.

This implied, however, a ratio of only one clergyman to about 1,750 members of the Church of Ireland, and Belfast remained a great problem. In 1928 the general synod set up a commission empowered to advance loans to assist church building in Belfast, and nine parishes received grants. In 1938, as a result of vigorous pressure from the bishop and diocesan council, the general synod agreed to grant £40,000 towards the cost of building churches and parish halls in Belfast. By 1940 grants had been made to fourteen parishes (about one-third of the cost being met by parochial and diocesan subscriptions). In addition, in 1912 the Trinity College, Dublin, mission in Belfast, with Arthur Barton, a future archbishop of Dublin at its head, started work in the immense parish of St Mary's in Belfast, and eighteen years later the southern church mission, supported by a grant from the general synod and by subscriptions from each of the dioceses south of the border, was placed in Ballymacarrett in east Belfast, with the aim of helping the church 'to concentrate upon one of the areas where the population is most crowded and where the ranks of the workers are thin'.[7]

For about ten years there was stability, but in the mid-1930s it was again urged that the changing population pattern required a reshaping of the parochial structure. In 1935 a committee was appointed by the general synod to consider the question of clerical mobility (more frequent movement amongst beneficed clergymen). This committee not only suggested that the patronage in every third avoidance should be exercised by the bishop, but also went on to emphasize that reforms suggested in 1920 – drastic changes in parochial boundaries and compulsory superannuation – had 'since become so urgent that the church can no longer adopt a leisurely attitude toward them'. Again, the pressures produced by a great war hastened the pace of ecclesiastical reorganization. By the mid-1940s the clergy again found themselves members of a fixed income group facing inflation, and the representative church body had to cope with a situation dominated by rising prices and cheap money (which meant a relatively poor return on its investments). In 1947 a bold step was taken, the representative church body being authorized to invest in the debentures, preference or ordinary shares of any company incorporated in Great Britain or Ireland. Advised by a firm of merchant bankers, the representative body began to move into equities and, by 1966, of its total capital, 11 per cent was in preference and 36 per cent in ordinary shares. By then its income had increased by 70 per cent from the 1946 level, amounting to £825,800, and its net assets amounted to £16,000,000.

At the same time efforts were made to raise stipends. In 1948 the minimum stipend for an incumbent was fixed at £450 and for a curate at £250–£280. In less than ten years these minima were found to be insufficient, and in 1957 the minimum for a incumbent was raised to £750, and for a curate to £400. In addition grants were made towards 'locomotory' expenses, incurred in the performance of parochial duties. In 1962 the minimum for an incumbent was again raised to £850, and in 1965 to £950, when the minimum for a curate was fixed at £600. About 1960 the salary of a secondary school master in the Irish republic ranged from £600 to £1,200, and in Northern Ireland from £600, to £1,600.[8] It should be added that in the previous year a superannuation scheme was introduced which provided that no clergyman should hold ecclesiastical office in the Church of Ireland after reaching the age of 75.

As in the past, the question of clerical incomes was clearly related to the distribution of clerical manpower, and in 1956 the general synod appointed a small committee of experienced administrators to the sparsely populated areas committee to survey both 'the really sparsely populated areas, where there were long distances between Church of Ireland families', and the areas where there were more churches than were required with modern travel facilities. The commissioners, who worked for years, found in the areas they surveyed 344 cures, which by arrangement they reduced to 256 with 743 churches. They recommended that 144 churches should be closed and allocated a number of grants for new 'economical and easily run' rectories. Partly as a result of this Beeching-style operation, by 1965 there was a considerable reduction of benefices in every diocese except the dioceses of Down and Dromore and Connor (the number of benefices in these dioceses having increased from 161 in 1925 to 190). In 1925 there were 974 benefices, by 1965 there were only 725. Of these about 300 were in Northern Ireland, but since about three-quarters of the curates in the Church of Ireland were working in the six counties, the total clerical manpower of the churches was divided roughly equally between the Republic of Ireland and Northern Ireland. Of the 25 parishes which by 1968 had obtained advances from a fund set up in 1959 by the general synod to provide loans for churches and church halls in new housing areas, 23 were in the dioceses of Down and Connor. In 1945 the population balance was to some extent acknowledged by separating the diocese of Connor, which covered Antrim, from Down and Connor.

The required clerical manpower was being recruited by new methods. The First World War led to a fall in the number of divinity students in Trinity College, Dublin, but by the 1930s there was a distinct improvement in the position, an annual average of approximately thirty-five men securing the testimonium, an output sufficient for the church's requirements. In the 1940s, however, there was a downward trend in the membership of the divinity school and by the 1960s this had reached the point where the annual average of testimonia granted had fallen to about ten. Drastic steps were taken to meet the situation. A new machinery was set up which came into operation in 1961, with the aim of discovering and encouraging candidates from over a wide field. A panel of selectors, clerical and lay, was nominated by the bench of bishops and twice a year committees formed from this panel interviewed candidates, each of which had been nominated by the bishop of his diocese. Those selected were sent for training to the divinity hostel, which was moved to new and extensive premises in 1964. With an increased staff, which provided both theological teaching and instruction in pastoral work and the devotional life, it was transformed into a theological college from which a rising proportion of the candidates for ordination in the Church of Ireland are being drawn, the students still taking divinity lectures and graduating in Dublin university.

It is comparatively easy to outline changes in the ecclesiastical framework and developments in financial policy, but there are other aspects of a church's life, which are both more important and harder to summarize and assess. It is, too, in handling these aspects that a shortening of the historical perspective makes it much more difficult to assign proportion and significance. A quick survey suggests that until the middle of the century the Church of Ireland responded cautiously to the demands imposed by changing circumstances. It was a small church in a small country. Its leadership was largely composed of people who were closely connected not only in their work for their church, but by family ties, social contacts and often by a common educational background. The clergy, still almost to a man Trinity Dublin graduates, were often sons of the rectory, a fact strikingly, exemplified by the existence of celebrated episcopal dynasties who gave devoted service, Greggs, Croziers, Days and Peacockes. And many of the leading laymen belonged to the intricately connected families of the landed gentry or to well-known professional and business families. Inevitably, then, the Church of Ireland was a church of tenacious loyalties, and a reverence for tradition.

It is significant that for about forty years, beginning in the 1920s, the Church of Ireland was led (or some would say dominated) by John Allen Fitzgerald Gregg, archbishop successively of Dublin and Armagh, who might fairly be described as an instinctive conservative with, however, an awareness of contemporary trends which made him not unresponsive to demands for change. Gregg's bearing suggested a prince of the church or at least a prelate of the establishment – he once recalled with melancholy pride that his grandfather had sat in the house of lords as bishop of Cork. He was a scholar, and a man of affairs, his administrative flair being reinforced by dignity, decisiveness and a sardonic wit (protecting an intense shyness). His theological sympathies were high church, though he had been brought up an evangelical and had an Anglo-Irish distaste for ceremonial exuberance. Gregg's profound sincerity of conviction, clarity of expression and unswerving devotion to his church gave him, as time went on, a remarkable weight in its councils and an immeasurable influence on its life.[9]

While Gregg was archbishop of Dublin, the Church of Ireland was working in a country where, if constitutional politics be exempted, the pace of change was slow. Only in about 1939 in the north, and somewhat later in the twenty-six counties, did the speed of economic advance accelerate in a marked degree. But this, together with changes in economic organization, increased emigration, which led to continuous coming and going between the two islands, urban re-shaping, rising standards of living with, notably in Northern Ireland, improved

social services and the advent of broadcasting and television, all
had incalculable effects on Irish life. Ireland became in a
marked degree an outward-looking country at the time when
the comparative isolation and intensive local life which had
been typical of so many districts in Ireland was being broken
down.

That conditions were changing was brought home to the
general synod at its first post-war meeting, when archbishop
Gregg pointed out that

in a parochial population of say a thousand, there will be found a
small number of individuals, say fifteen to twenty-five per cent, which
remains constant year after year, while the rest of the population, and
by far the larger part of it in most cases, consists of those who
occasionally go to church down to those who never go.

Never before had the distinction between denominational
statistics and active church membership been emphasized so
authoritatively in the general synod. What is noteworthy,
however, is that during the post-war years the Church of Ireland
was making decided efforts to discover new means by which it
might effectively influence Irish society. The diocese and the
parish continued to provide the structural framework for the
greater part of the church's work. It was the parish church and
hall round which clustered the societies and clubs, in which
there were focused the different activities of the church,
religious, educational, charitable, missionary and recreational.
The intensity of parish life remained very strong, and this was
partly responsible for an important constitutional change,
implemented by legislation at the beginning of the twenties and
the close of the forties. Women always played a big part in the
life of the parish, even if excluded from the councils of the
church, and in 1920 this was acknowledged when they were
admitted to vestries and made eligible for membership of select
vestries (with careful provision that not more than one half
the membership of any select vestry should be women). Then,
in 1949, women were made eligible for all lay offices in the
church.

But though parochial life remained the recognized focus of
much of the church's work and influence, during the post-war
years the Church of Ireland showed that it was aware of

important spheres in which the church must work by the building of a church at Shannon airport (its use being shared with presbyterians and methodists), by the appointment of an industrial officer and an educational officer, by the formation of a committee on broadcasting and television, and by encouraging pastoral work in Queen's University, Belfast, (where by the mid-1950s there were nearly 1,000 Church of Ireland students) – by the appointment of a whole-time chaplain, the provision of an annual course of theological lectures by a visiting theologian and the foundation of a students' centre, to which in the 1960s a church and hall were added.

During the post-war decades important developments occurred in two most important aspects of the church's life, liturgical worship and reunion. After the vigorous revision controversies of the 1870s, the Church of Ireland had abstained from large-scale liturgical debates for a generation. Then in 1909 the general synod had appointed a prayer book committee. This committee's aims were 'to enrich and at the same time to simplify the public devotions of our church and to render the language used more generally intelligible'. It set to work vigorously, producing within two years of its appointment 120 pages of recommendations, and its proposals were embodied in a series of enactments which took effect in 1926. One of these, it may be said was a frank confession that the commission had made mistakes – a statute for the elimination of 'certain infelicities of diction' in the revised text of the prayer book. Though it made a number of minor verbal changes, this revision was basically conservative in spirit.[10] But in the 1950s there were signs of a growing desire for a more radical re-shaping and re-wording of the liturgy. In 1956 a shortening of the services was permitted, and in 1962 a liturgical advisory committee was set up which both replanned the principal services of the church and began 'the all important work of phrasing in current English the language of the different services'.[11] In 1967 the general synod authorized the use for an experimental period, of any service produced by the liturgical advisory committee. These services have so far aroused much interest, even if they have failed to give universal satisfaction. Though the revision now in progress has been pronounced the most radical so far undertaken by the Church of Ireland, 'a note of conservatism

. . . is still plain to be seen in the retention of the main characteristics of 1662'.

It may be added that the discussions over to what extent liturgical revision to accord with current trends should be carried almost completely overshadowed the old argument over ritualism. In 1926 the incumbent of St Bartholomew's, Dublin, was found guilty in the court of the general synod of turning his back on the people during public prayers, of bowing to the holy table and of using lighted candles when not required for the purpose of illumination; and ten years later the ceremonial practices of the vicar of St John's, Sandymount, led to protracted litigation, the vicar at one stage trying to secure from the high court an order of prohibition directed to the court of the general synod, forbidding it to hear the case or take cognizance of the charges against him, on the grounds that St John's was a trustee church. The high court refused to issue the order and in the event the court of the general synod found him guilty of twenty out of the twenty-one counts on which he was accused. But by the 1960s the atmosphere had so greatly changed that the much-debated canon thirty-six, which forbade the placing of a cross on the holy table, was in 1964 repealed.

At the beginning of the 1920s the outlook for reunion had seemed hopeful, at least to an optimistic broad churchman. At the 1921 session of the general synod, the primate, D'Arcy, comparing the Lambeth conference of the previous year with that of 1908, said that he was conscious of 'a wider outlook, a great readiness to fraternise and listen to voices coming from outside their own communion', and five years later D'Arcy saw 'the icy exclusiveness cherished by many in the past and maintained by some extreme partizans in the present . . . melting in the sunshine of a growing Christian charity'. There was some justification for D'Arcy's optimism. In 1921 the general synod had appointed 23 January as a day of intercession for Christian unity. In 1922 representatives of the Church of Ireland and the presbyterian church in Ireland were authorized to begin to try and formulate proposals which might lead to unity. Finally, inspired probably by the great conference on faith and order at Athens in 1927, at which the Church of Ireland was of course represented, the home reunion committee of the general synod surveyed the Irish situation with the aim of discovering how, within the immediate future, a greater degree of Christian unity could be attained. Recognizing that 'the only unity policy of the Church of Rome is that of complete absorption in its own system', the committee decided that 'the most statesmanlike line of approach for the Church of Ireland' was towards an understanding with the presbyterian church which might prevent a wasteful overlapping of effort in the south and west of Ireland and which might ultimately lead to an organic union. Encouraged by conferences between members of the Church of Ireland and members of the Irish presbyterian church, held in Armagh and Dublin in 1931, the general synod appointed a committee to meet representatives of the Irish presbyterian church to consider the question of reunion in Ireland. The representatives met, and in 1935 the home reunion committee asked the general synod to agree to a report affirming that the Church of Ireland 'fully and freely recognizes the validity, efficacy and spiritual reality of both ordination and sacraments as administered in the presbyterian church'. The archbishop of Dublin, Gregg, moved an amendment stating that the synod recognized with regret that approach to reunion in Ireland along the lines laid down by the Lambeth conference 'offers no present prospect of union'. And D'Arcy accepted this amendment as a preferable alternative to the downright rejection of the report.

Ten years later the general synod's Christian unity committee admitted that 'we cannot record any overt moves toward organic union in our country'. However, shortly afterwards, the Church of Ireland entered into closer relations with non-anglican bodies outside Ireland. In 1950 it agreed to inter-communion with the old catholic churches; in 1956 it recognized the orders of the church of South India; in 1963 it established full communion with the Spanish reformed and Lusitanian churches and the independent Philippine church. In 1964 the general synod approved of the invitation of discussions with the presbyterian and methodist churches in Ireland 'with a view to Christian unity'; in 1968 representatives of the Church of Ireland and the methodist and presbyterian churches in Ireland met for discussions; and in 1960 a significant gesture was made towards the largest denomination in Ireland when Ballinahinch church in the diocese of Tuam, which had been closed, was handed over to the Roman catholic diocese of Tuam.

The active interest shown by the leaders of the Church of Ireland in Christian unity reflects their awareness of the forces at work in contemporary Christianity. From the beginning of what it was optimistically believed could be called the post-war era (the years between 1918 and 1939), the Church of Ireland was becoming steadily involved in international and inter-denominational thought and action. The Lambeth conference of 1920 approved of the formation of councils of churches to consider matters affecting social and moral welfare. In 1922 the general synod approved of the establishment of such a council in Ireland and in 1923 the united council of Christian churches and religious communities in Ireland was formed (from 1965 the Irish council of churches). The Church of Ireland representatives played an active part in the workings of the united council which both expressed the views of the Irish protestant churches on social issues and arranged for Irish representation at church conferences, both in Great Britain and overseas.

From shortly after its foundation, it was deeply concerned over unemployment and world peace. In 1926 it declared that much could be done 'to revive trade by frank and friendly co-operation between capital and labour'. Some years later it called on governments to undertake 'productive rather than luxury expenditure' and asked Christian people 'to see to it that whatever money is at their disposal . . . is used as far as possible for the purchase of those commodities which in their production provide the largest amount of labour'. The council welcomed the Kellogg pact and requested the educational authorities in the Irish Free State and Northern Ireland 'to take steps to introduce into the teaching of the schools the subjects of World peace and the work of the League of nations'. The Northern Ireland minister of education replied that a circular on the importance of the league of nations had been issued to primary schools. The Free State minister of education acknowledged the receipt of the council's request. In 1934 it adopted a statement defining its attitude to war which reflected contemporary pacifist opinion. The statement not only declared that war was incompatible with Christ's teaching, but urged churches to declare that they would refuse to support their government if it engaged in war in defiance of the Kellogg pact or the league of nations, or if it had refused to submit the matter in dispute to arbitration. When the united council's report was placed before the general synod, that body, after a vigorous debate, decided to 'receive' the report but refused to 'commend' the views expressed in it to Irish churchmen. In the years preceding the outbreak of war in 1939, the council was also concerned over housing in Dublin and was pressing for legislation to protect women and children, and to check intemperance. (It was better pleased with the Northern Ireland act of 1923 than with the Free State measure of 1927.) Viewing with great concern the growth of gambling, it strongly disapproved 'on moral as well as patriotic grounds' of the hospital sweepstake, which was one of the great sources of support for hospital development in the south. After the war ended in 1945, the council encouraged the churches it represented to raise large sums for the churches in devastated Europe and in 1955 it set up a hostel for refugees.

The council's reports show an ever-increasing concern with enlarging and strengthening the Irish churches' contacts with international Christian organizations, and the Church of Ireland was represented at gatherings such as COPEC in 1924 and the Oxford conference on church, community and state in 1937, and on permanent bodies such as the British council of churches and the world council of churches.

As the centenary of the Irish church act approached, the Church of Ireland was actively engaged in participating in international Christian movements, in reorganizing its resources to meet changing circumstances (an activity at which it had become adept) and, as the primate expressed it at the general synod of 1968, in preparing 'to make contact with people who are thinking in the manner of the twentieth century'. But events were to show that in the part of Ireland where the great majority of the adherents of the Church of Ireland lived passions associated with earlier centuries were still strong.

NOTES

<hr />

CHAPTER I THE CHURCH OF IRELAND IN THE MID-NINETEENTH
CENTURY

1 28 Geo. III c. 32.
2 U. H. H. de Burgh, *The landowners of Ireland*, Dublin, 1878.
3 A. Trollope, *Last chronicle of Barset*, chapter 58.
4 G. A. Birmingham, *Irishmen all*, London, 1913, p. 109.
5 *Authorised report of the church congress held at Dublin*, Dublin, 1868, p. 131.
6 *The Times*, 28 December 1885.
7 *Irish ecclesiastical gazette*, 7 March 1890.
8 *Irish ecclesiastical gazette*, 21 April 1890.
9 *Saturday Review*, 14 October 1863.
10 M. Trench, *Richard Chenevix Trench, archbishop: letters and memorials*, London, 1888, i, p. 340.
11 R. C. Trench, *A charge . . .*, Dublin, 1875, p. 20.
12 W. Sherlock, 'The story of the revision of the Irish prayer book', in *Irish church quarterly*, iii, p. 27.
13 Clarendon to Gladstone, 2 January 1869 (Add. MS 44133).
14 W. G. Carroll, *A memoir of the Rt Rev. James Thomas O'Brien*, Dublin, 1875.
15 I. Madden, *Memoir of the Rt Rev. Robert Daly*, London, 1875.
16 R. S. Gregg, *Memorials of the life of John Gregg*, Dublin, 1879, pp. 67, 121, 209–10. Todd, a high churchman, said that the characteristics of Gregg's pupil style were 'a very rapid elocution, great gesticulation and repeating the same thing over and over again in slightly varied language' (Todd to Wilberforce, 22 January 1862).
17 A vast amount of information relating to clerical incomes and the size of parishes is contained in the *Report of Her Majesty's commissioners on the revenues and condition of the established church (Ireland), and appendix* (3956, 4082), H.C. 1867–8, xxiv.

18 E. Maguire, *Fifty years of clerical life in the Church of Ireland*, Dublin, 1904.
19 S. Butcher, *A charge* . . ., Dublin, 1867, pp. 31–3.
20 Though the dean's salary and the expenses of the chapel were included in the vote for the viceregal household, it was argued that the chapel was the king's chapel in Ireland and not a viceregal chapel. In 1922 the archbishop of Armagh was anxious that the chapel should be maintained at the expense of the crown or the British government as an 'expression of the fact that the monarchy is a Christian institution'. But the funds were not forthcoming and in 1944 the Irish Free State government handed over the building to the Roman catholic church (Davidson papers, 1922 (10)).
21 National Library of Ireland, MS 11216(2).
22 *Dublin university commission report* . . . (1637, 1017), H.C. 1852–3, xlv, pp. 18–25, 73–4, 285–7, 301.
23 *Athenaeum*, 19 May 1883.
24 Salmon to Reichel, 3 August 1893 (Salmon letters, T.C.D.).
25 F. R. Wynne, *Spent in the service: a memoir of the Very Rev. Achilles Daunt*, London, 1879.
26 *Authorised report of the church congress held in Dublin*, Dublin, 1868, p. 122.
27 W. Fitzgerald, *Duties of the parochial clergy: a charge*, London, 1857, p. 75.
28 A. Trollope, *Clergymen of the Church of England*, London, 1866, p. 116.
29 Warburton to Gladstone, 24 March 1868 (Add. MS 44414).
30 *Saturday Review*, 7 March 1868.
31 Annals of Christ Church, Belfast, from its foundation in 1831 (PRONI, T 1075/11).
32 D. Alcock, *Walking with God: a memoir of the Venerable John Alcock*, London, 1886.
33 A. G. Dann, *George Webster: a memoir*, Dublin, 1892; G. Webster, *An address to the parishioners of Saint Nicholas*, Cork, 1863; G. Webster, *Amusements: a lecture*, Dublin, 1859.
34 J. T. O'Brien, *The case of the established church in Ireland*, Dublin, 1867, note F.
35 *Royal commission of inquiry into primary education (Ireland)*, vol. viii, H.C. 1870 [C 6 vii], pp. 34–56, xxviii.
36 H. K. Moore, *The centenary book*, Dublin, 1911, p. 27; reports of the church education society.
37 J. Godkin, *Ireland and her churches*, London, 1867, p. 509.
38 M. MacColl, *Memoirs and correspondence*, ed. G. W. E. Russell, London, 1914.
39 *Journal of the general synod*, 1905, pp. lxvii–viii.

CHAPTER II DISESTABLISHMENT

1 G. M. Trevelyan, *Life of John Bright*, London, 1913, p. 161.
2 *Hansard 3*, cxxxv, 116–39, 1138–84, cxxxv, 418–32, clxx, 1988–2020, clxxi, 457–7, 1560–90, 1675–1716, clxxviii, 384–455.

3 A. C. Ewald, *Life and letters of Sir Joseph Napier*, 2nd ed., London, 1892, pp. 244–50.

4 J. T. O'Brien, *The case of the established church of Ireland*, Dublin, 1867, p. 7.

5 M. G. Beresford, *A charge*, Dublin, 1868, p. 24.

6 C. B. Bernard, *A primary charge*, Dublin, 1861.

7 W. Lee, *The position and prospects of the Church of Ireland*, Dublin, 1867, p. 14.

8 *Contemporary Review*, vii, pp. 429–44; J. C. MacDonnell, *Life and correspondence of W. C. Magee*, 1896, i, p. 160.

9 E. A. Stopford, *To the clergy and laity*, Dublin, 1868, p. 5; the primate to Lord Mayo, 2 June 1867, enclosing draft of bill (N.L.I. MS 11216, 1, 2).

10 *Convocation (Ireland) . . . Copies of letters from His Grace the archbishop of Armagh to Her Majesty's secretary of state for the home department . . .* 562, H.C. 1864, xliv; W. Fitzgerald, *The revival of synods*, London, 1861, pp. 9–12.

11 *Irish ecclesiastical gazette*, 19 August 1868. Two distinguished lawyers, Palmer and A. J. Stephens, were of the opinion that the royal permission was not required (*Irish ecclesiastical gazette*, 20 October 1868).

12 Printed reports of the proceedings of the conferences of the clergy are in the diocesan office, Belfast.

13 *Hansard 3*, clvii, 159; clviii, 422–3; cxc, 1390–1.

14 W. F. Monypenny and G. E. Buckle, *Life of Benjamin Disraeli*, v, London, 1920, p. 119; A. R. Ashwell and R. G. Wilberforce, *Life of the Rt Rev. Samuel Wilberforce*, London, 1882, iii, p. 42.

15 *Hansard 3*, cxci, 472.

16 W. F. Monypenny and G. E. Buckle, *Life of Benjamin Disraeli*, iii, pp. 15, 18.

17 A. E. Gathorne-Hardy, *Gathorne Hardy, first earl of Cranbrook*, 2 vols, London, 1910, i, p. 268.

18 *The Times*, 7 May 1868; Napier to Tait, 7 May 1868 (Tait papers).

19 M. Trench, *Richard Chenevix Trench, archbishop: letters and memorials*, 1888, ii, p. 55; J. C. MacDonnell, *Life and correspondence of W. C. Magee*, i, pp. 180, 182.

20 W. F. Monypenny and G. E. Buckle, *Life of Benjamin Disraeli*, v, pp. 60–8; *Letters of Queen Victoria*, 2nd series, i, pp. 533–9; Napier to Cairns (c. 1858) (Cairns papers); J. C. MacDonnell, *Life and correspondence of W. C. Magee*, i, p. 150.

21 Gladstone to J. Pooler, 26 May 1896 (R.C.B. Library); Memorandum for Queen (Add. MS 44757).

22 *Irish ecclesiastical gazette*, 18 February 1869; M. Trench, *Richard Chenevix Trench, archbishop: letters and memorials*, ii, p. 73; *Hansard 3*, cxvi, 1810.

23 R. Palmer, *Memorials*, pt ii, pp. 114, 119; notes of conversations, C.S.R., 1 January 1869 (Add. MS 44306).

24 Stopford to Gladstone, 6 February 1869 (Add. MS 44419).

25 R. B. O'Brien, *Life of Charles Stewart Parnell*, London, 1898, ii, p. 362.

26 Gladstone to Sullivan, 7 January 1869, Sullivan to Gladstone, 6 January, 4 February 1869, Stopford to Gladstone, 31 January 1867 (Add. MSS 44418, 44419).

27 Atkins to Gladstone, July 1869, MacDonnell to Gladstone, 12 April 1869 (Add. MS 44420); Knox to Gladstone, 6 October 1868 (Add. MS 44416); Knox to Tait, 13 February 1869 (Tait papers).

28 J. C. MacDonnell, *Life and correspondence of W. C. Magee*, i, p. 211.

29 Ibid., pp. 215–17; A. R. Ashwell and R. G. Wilberforce, *Life of the Rt Rev. Samuel Wilberforce*, 1882, iii, pp. 283–6.

30 R. T. Davidson and W. Benham, *Life of Archibald Campbell Tait*, London, 1891, ii, pp. 12–14; Tait to Grey, 4 March 1869 (Tait papers).

31 Wilberforce to Gladstone, 16 February 1869, Gladstone to Granville, 6 January 1869 (Add. MS 44166).

32 *The Times*, 25, 26, 27 February 1869.

33 Minutes of the consultative committee, 11 November 1868–6 April 1869 (R.C.B. papers).

34 Beresford to Napier, 3 March 1869 (R.C.B. letters); Napier's opinion is in Minutes of consultative committee.

35 *Irish Times*, 13, 14 April 1869.

36 Minute book of the standing committee of the church conference, 16 April–30 July 1869 (R.C.B. papers).

37 In committee changed to ten years.

38 *Queen Victoria's letters*, 2nd series, ii, pp. 603–4.

39 J. C. MacDonnell, *Life and correspondence of W. C. Magee*, i, pp. 225–6.

40 *Irish Times*, 31 May 1869.

41 J. C. MacDonnell, *Life and correspondence of W. C. Magee*, i, p. 227; Cairns to Tait, —— 1869; C. J. Ellicott to Tait, 5 June 1869 (Tait papers); *The Times*, 7 June 1869.

42 J. C. MacDonnell, *Life and correspondence of W. C. Magee*, i, p. 228; *The Times*, 16 June 1869; *Queen Victoria's letters*, 2nd series, ii, pp. 609–10.

43 *Queen Victoria's letters*, 2nd series, ii, p. 604.

44 Gladstone to Granville, 18 July 1869 (Add. MS 44166).

45 J. C. MacDonnell, *Life and correspondence of W. C. Magee*, i, pp. 233–4.

46 Granville to Gladstone, 21 July 1867 (Add. MS 44166). Account of negotiations by Granville, dated 4 August 1869 (Add. MS 44166).

47 *Report of the commissioners of church temporalities in Ireland for 1875*, [C 1400], 1876, xx, pp. 4–6.

48 Plunket to T. Green, 19 July 1869 (R.C.B. letters).

49 J. H. Bernard, *Archbishop Benson in Ireland*, London, 1896.

CHAPTER III   RECONSTRUCTION

1 *The national synod of the Church of Ireland*: the synods of Armagh and Dublin, September 1869/70, together with the *Journal of the lower house of the united synods*, Dublin, 1869.

2 *Irish Times*, 13, 31 August 1869.

3 W. Bence Jones to Tait, 21 October 1869 (Tait papers).

4 *Irish Times*, 13, 14, 15 October 1869.

5 Minute book of the general committee appointed in conformity with the resolutions of the lay conference.

6 W. Sherlock, *Church organization*, Dublin, 1868.

7 Supply of clergy committee papers (representative church body, Library MS a/4).

8 Salmon to —— ——, September 1894 (Salmon letters, T.C.D.); H. R. Reichel, *Sermons of Charles Parsons Reichel*, London, 1899, p. lvii.

9 R. C. Trench, *A charge* . . ., 1871, p. 49; *Irish ecclesiastical gazette*, 21 June 1871.

10 *Principles at stake: essays on church questions of the day*, ed. G. H. Sumner, London, 1868, p. 235.

11 J. Gregg, *A charge* . . ., 2nd ed., Dublin, 1867, p. 40.

12 *Dublin Daily Express*, April 1866.

13 A. H. Dawson, *A short account of St Bartholomew's church*, Dublin, 1871; *Daily Express*, 3, 6, 8 January 1868, 26 December 1867.

14 C. F. D'Arcy, *Adventures of a bishop*, London, 1934, p. 35; M. Petre, *The autobiography and life of George Tyrrell*, Dublin, 1911, i, p. 97; *Irish Times*, 27 June, 13 September 1872; *Athenaeum*, 9 July 1887.

15 M. Trench, *Richard Chenevix Trench, archbishop: letters and memorials*, ii, pp. 125–31; *Daily Express*, 13, 19 April, 18 May 1872.

16 G. Salmon, *Thoughts on the present crisis in the Church of Ireland*, Dublin, 1870.

17 For character sketches of the leading figures in the revision debates, see W. Sherlock, 'The story of the revision of the Irish prayer book', *Irish church quarterly*, iii, pp. 12–32, 144–66.

18 J. O. Hannay, *Pleasant places*, London, 1934, p. 54.

19 *Irish ecclesiastical gazette*, 22 June 1875, and supplement, May 1877.

20 E. Alexander, *Primate Alexander* . . ., London, 1913, p. 188.

21 *Irish ecclesiastical gazette*, May 1872.

22 J. Napier, *Speech . . . delivered at . . . the general synod . . . 21 May 1873*, Dublin, 1873, p. 10.

23 *Church of Ireland gazette*, 12 October 1917.

24 M. Trench, *Richard Chenevix Trench* . . ., ii, p. 172.

25 *Irish Times*, 1 March 1870.

26 *Journal of the general synod* . . ., 1881, appendix, p. 69.

27 Trench pessimistically expected that a number of the clergy, 'little used to having money', would be demoralized if they were given capital grants (Trench to Wilberforce, 21 November 1868).

28 *Journal of the general synod* . . ., 1876, appendix, p. 75.

29 S. Gwynn, *Ulster*, 1911, p. 31.

30 *Journal of the general synod* . . ., 1880, appendix, p. 49; *Representative body of the church of Ireland: appeal in aid of the church sustentation fund*, 1870, p. 3.

31 For an account of the work accomplished by the representative church body between 1871 and 1880, see *Journal of the general synod* . . ., 1871, appendix, pp. 67–95.

32 L. Robinson, *Palette and plough*, Dublin, 1948, p. 34.

33 *Irish church quarterly*, i, p. 3.

CHAPTER IV   THE FIRST FORTY YEARS OF DISESTABLISHMENT

1 H. H. Henson, *Retrospect of an unimportant life*, ii, p. 130.
2 A. C. Benson, *Life of Edward White Benson, sometime archbishop of Canterbury*, 2 vols, London, 1899, ii, p. 725.
3 *Viceregal committee on intermediate education in Ireland* [Cmd 66], p. 13, H.C. 1919, xx.
4 L. Fleming, *Head or harp*, London, 1965, p. 22.
5 *The authorised report of the church of Ireland conference held at Limerick*, 1902, pp. 180–1.
6 G. A. Birmingham, *Irishmen all*, London, 1913, pp. 193–207.
7 J. O. Hannay, *The life of Frederick Richards Wynne*, London, 1897, pp. 47, 117.
8 *Third and final report of the Belfast church extension society . . . including a short review of its history*, 1925.
9 H. M. Thompson and F. J. Bigger, *The cathedral church of Belfast*, Belfast, 1923.
10 *Irish ecclesiastical gazette*, 19 March, 9 April, 28 May 1887, 21 January, 7 April 1898.
11 'Nomad', quoted in R. S. Breene, *The golden jubilee book of Saint Peter's Church, Belfast. 1900–1950*, Belfast, 1950.
12 T. Cooke-Trench, *An autobiography to which is appended an account of the church of Saint Michael and All Angels at Clane*, Galway, n.d.
13 G. E. Street, *The cathedral of the Holy Trinity called Christ Church . . . an account of the restoration of the fabric*, London, 1882.
14 *Dublin Evening Mail*, 3 May 1878; *Irish ecclesiastical gazette*, December 1894. The cathedral and synod hall were said to have cost Roe £200,000 and 'a turn in the tide of property having taken place', this proved 'a source of embarrassment' to his firm (*The Times*, 26 November 1894).
15 J. G. F. Day and H. E. Patton, *The cathedrals of the Church of Ireland*, Dublin, 1932.
16 *Irish ecclesiastical gazette*, 31 October 1890. Thomas Mills, incumbent of St Jude's, Dublin (d. 1900), is said to have been the last man in the Church of Ireland habitually to preach in a black gown.
17 *Hansard 3*, lxxxviii, p. 63; *Dublin University petitions . . .*, H.C. 1872 (41), xvii; *Journal of the general synod . . .*, 1878, appendix, pp. 133–9; *Journal of the general synod . . .*, 1880, appendix, pp. 80–4; *Hansard 3*, cc, 1097–1113.
18 *Dictionary of national biography*, and *Church of Ireland gazette*, 13 April 1917.
19 N. J. D. White, *John Henry Bernard*, Dublin, 1928, p. 4. See also R. H. Murray, *Archbishop Bernard: professor, prelate, provost*, London, 1931.
20 *Royal commission on Trinity College, Dublin . . . appendix to the final report*, pp. 362–72, [Cd 3312], H.C. 1907, xli; *Church of England yearbook*, p. 134; *Irish church quarterly*, vi, p. 192.

21 *Royal commission on ecclesiastical discipline, minutes of evidence* [Cd 3096], pp. 231–40, H.C. 1906, xxxiii.

22 *Ritualism in the diocese of Dublin: a correspondence between the protestant defence association and the archbishop of Dublin* (Dublin).

23 *Journal of the general synod,* 1890, xliv; *Journal of the general synod,* 1893, p. vi.

24 *Church of Ireland gazette,* 16 February 1900; 21 October 1904.

25 *Hansard 4,* lxvii, 1223, lxviii, 26, 947, 1320, lxix, 647, lxxv, 91; *Church of Ireland gazette,* 23 February, 2 March 1900; J. Boyle, 'The Belfast protestant association and the independent Orange order 1901–10', in *Irish Historical Studies,* xii, pp. 117–52.

26 Smyth (d. 1932) in 1907 became rector of St George's, Montreal.

27 Peacocke papers (PRONI mic. 87).

28 *Journal of the general synod . . .,* 1908, appendix, pp. 213–14; *Journal of the general synod . . .,* 1911, lxxvi.

29 *Journal of the general synod . . .,* 1915, appendix, pp. 402–4; *Journal of the general synod . . .,* 1917, appendix, pp. 330–2.

30 R. M. Gwynn, E. M. Norton and B. W. Simpson, *'T.C.D.' in China: a history of the Dublin University Fukien mission, 1885–1935,* Dublin, 1936, *Light and Life,* Michaelmas 1952.

31 E. Chatterton, *The story of fifty years' mission work in Chota Nagpur,* London, 1901, and H. V. White, *List of SPG missionaries, 1701–1895, of Irish parentage,* 1895.

32 C. F. Harford Battersley, *Pilkington of Uganda,* London, 1899.

33 *Journal of the general synod . . .,* 1914, appendix, pp. 290–9.

34 For correspondence on the Spanish church question see, 'The Spanish and Portuguese reformed episcopal churches', a collection of letters, pamphlets, etc. (R.C.B. Library); F. D. How, *William Conyngham Plunket . . . a memoir,* London, 1900, chs 14–18; G. Seaver, *John Allen Fitzgerald Gregg: archbishop,* London, 1963, ch. 8; *The Times,* 3 August 1966; *Freeman's Journal,* 27 September 1894; *Church Times,* 12 October 1894; J. G. Snead-Cox, *Life of cardinal Vaughan,* ii, London, 1910, pp. 164–74.

CHAPTER V   THE CHURCH AND IRISH POLITICS

1 *Journal of the general synod . . .,* 1893, pp. xiv–lii, C. S. Parnell to Galbraith, n.d.

2 R. B. Knox to Galbraith, 28, 31 December 1888, 11, 20 January *Irish Times.*

3 J. O. Hannay to Montgomery, 1907 (Montgomery papers, PRONI).

4 *The seething pot,* 1905, pp. 37, 134.

5 For a perceptive account of Hannay's outlook and his relations with Irish nationalism see R. B. D. French, 'J. O. Hannay and the Gaelic League', in *Hermathena,* cii, pp. 26–52.

6 T. W. Rolleston to Hannay, 12 March 1905 (Hannay correspondence).

7 *Church of Ireland gazette,* 4 March 1904.

8 The bishop of Clogher to Mrs Hannay, 21 September 1905 (Hannay correspondence).

9 *Church of Ireland gazette*, 25 March 1904, 16 March 1906, 5 June 1908, 30 March 1917.
10 Minute books of the Cumann Gaodhalach na h-Eaglaise.
11 Peacocke to Bernard, 1, 5, 13, 14 September 1912 (Add. MS 52782). In fact Saturday 21st was the day of intercession appointed by the primate (*Irish Times*, 21 October 1912).
12 *Irish Times*, 1 October 1912.
13 *Church of Ireland gazette*, 24 October 1913; *Irish Times*, 28 October 1913; R. M. Fox, *History of the Irish Citizen Army*, Dublin, 1944, pp. 44–5.
14 *Church of Ireland gazette*, 4 September 1914.
15 *Church of Ireland gazette*, 24 September, 5, 19 November 1915, 29 September 1916.
16 *Irish Times*, 10 October 1916.
17 Bernard to General Maxwell, 18 May 1916 (Add. MS 52782).
18 *Church of Ireland gazette*, 28 April–5 May 1916.
19 *The Times*, 5 May 1916; Bernard to Lloyd George, 3 June 1916 (Lloyd George papers, D); R. H. Murray, *Archbishop Bernard: professor, prelate, provost*, London, 1931, p. 232.
20 Bernard to H. Barber, 23 April 1918 (Add. MS 52783).
21 *Church of Ireland gazette*, 11, 13 May 1917.
22 *Church of Ireland gazette*, 5, 12, 19 May 1922; *Irish Times*, 13 May 1922.
23 E. J. Gwynn to Bernard, 6 September 1921 (Add. MS 52783).
24 *Irish Times*, 17 April 1912.
25 *Dail Eireann, official report*, xii, 155.
26 *Church of Ireland gazette*, 20 February, 26 May 1925.
27 *Seanad Eireann . . . official report*, iv, pp. 936, 450–2; *Dail Eireann . . . official report*, x, pp. 159–66.
28 *Dail Eireann: official report*, xxvii, pp. 635–6; *Seanad Eirann . . . official report*, xii, pp. 68, 78.
29 *Irish reports . . .*, 1951, pp. 1–47.
30 *Journal of the general synod . . .*, 1946, p. 182.
31 An Roinn Oideachais. 'Oideachas Náisiúnta Áireamh ar sgoileanna, leanbhaí sgoile, oidí, cursaí airgid agus neithe eile ag baint le hOideachas Náisúnta i geaitheamh na bliana 1922-23. Statistics relating to National Education in Saorstat Eireann for the year 1922–23', 1925, pp. 6–7.
32 *Journal of the general synod . . .*, 1967, appendix, p. 90.

CHAPTER VI   THE CHURCH IN THE TWENTIETH CENTURY

1 *Church of Ireland gazette*, 10 July 1914.
2 Ibid., 2, 21 March 1917; 14, 21 March 1919; 19 March 1920.
3 Ibid., 23 February 1917.
4 Ibid., 13 February, 9 April, 14, 20, 21 May 1920.
5 *Viceregal committee on intermediate education in Ireland*, 1919, pp. 14–18, 56.
6 *Church of Ireland gazette*, 25 June 1905, 11 January 1907, 6 August 1920.
7 Ibid., 13, 20, 27 February 1925; *Journal of the general synod*, 1931, p. 37.
8 For schoolmasters' salaries in Northern Ireland and the Republic of

Ireland see *Tribunal on teachers' salaries report* (Prl 87); *Salaries of teachers*, 1959, Cmd 403.

9 G. Seaver, *John Allen Fitzgerald Gregg: archbishop*, London, 1963. *Journal of the general synod* . . ., 1958, p. lxxxvii.

10 G. J. Cuming, *A history of anglican liturgy*, London, 1969, p. 240.

11 *Journal of the general synod* . . ., 1966, appendix, p. 173.

BIBLIOGRAPHY

~~~~~~

MANUSCRIPT SOURCES

LONDON

British Museum

    Bernard papers
    Gladstone papers

Public Record Office

    Cairns papers

Lambeth Palace Library

    Davidson papers
    Tait papers

DUBLIN

Trinity College Library

    Galbraith papers
    Hannay papers
    Salmon letters

Church of Ireland Library

Leslie transcripts of diocesan succession lists.
The Spanish and Portuguese reformed episcopal churches, a collection of letters, pamphlets, etc., 1879–96
The supply of clergy committee, 1878, A/4 minute books of the Cumann Gaodhalach na h-Eaglaise

Representative church body

Minutes of the consultative committee
Letters relating to disestablishment

BELFAST

Public Record Office

The annals of Christ Church, Belfast, from its foundation in 1831,
T 1075/11
Peacocke papers (mic. 87)

PRINTED MATERIALS

GOVERNMENT PUBLICATIONS

Dublin University commission report . . ., H.C. 1852, (1637, 1017), xiv
*Dublin University commission: report . . . together with appendices, containing
evidence, suggestions and correspondence,* H.C. 1852–3, (1637, 1017), xlv
*Report of Her Majesty's commissioners on the revenues and condition of the
established church (Ireland), and appendix,* H.C. 1867–8, (3956, 4082),
xxiv
*Convocation (Ireland) . . . copies of letters from His Grace the Archbishop of
Armagh to Her Majesty's secretary of state for the home department* . . ., H.C.
1864 (562), xliv
Census of Ireland for the year 1871: abstract of the enumerators' returns,
[C 375], H.C. 1871, lix
*Census of Ireland, 1871, pt 1: area, houses, and population: also the ages, civil
condition, occupations, birthplaces, religion and education of the people* [C 662],
H.C. 1872, lxvii, [C 873], H.C. 1873, lxxii, [C 964], H.C. 1874, lxxiv,
[C 1106], H.C. 1874, lxxiv
Endowed schools, Ireland, commission, report, vols 1 and 2 [C 2831], [C 2831–
2], H.C. 1881, xxxv
Census of Ireland for the year 1901, preliminary report . . . [Cd 613], H.C.
1901, xc
*Census of Ireland, 1901, pt 1: area, houses and population; also the ages, civil or
conjugal condition, occupations, birthplaces, religion and education of the
people* [Cd 847], (1058, 1123, 1059), H.C. 1902, cxxii–cxxviii
*Royal commission on Trinity College, Dublin, and the University of Dublin, first
report* [Cd 3174], *appendix to the first report* [Cd 3176], H.C. 1906, vii,
final report [Cd 3311], *and appendix to the final report* [Cd 3312], H.C.
1907, xii
Royal commission on ecclesiastical discipline, minutes of evidence [Cd 3069],
H.C. 1906, xxxiii
*Census of Ireland for the year 1911, preliminary report with abstracts of the
enumerators' summaries* [Cd 5691], H.C. 1911, lxxi
*Census returns for Ireland, 1911, showing area, houses and population; also the
ages, civil or conjugal condition, occupation, birthplaces, religions and education
of the people* [Cd 6049–52], H.C. 1912–13, cxiv–cxvii

Bibliography

Government of Northern Ireland, census of population, 1926, general report
Saorstát Éireann, census of population, 1926, general report
Government of Northern Ireland, census of population, 1961, general report

CHURCH OF IRELAND OFFICIAL PUBLICATIONS

Journal of the general convention of the Church of Ireland, first session, 1870 . . .,
ed. Rev. A. T. Lee, Dublin, 1870
Journal of the general convention of the Church of Ireland, second session, 1870 . .
ed. Rev. A. T. Lee, Dublin, 1871
Report of the committee appointed by the general convention of the Church of Ireland on 31st October 1870 . . ., Dublin, 1871
Journal of the general synod of the Church of Ireland, 1871. In the appendix to the journal there are annually printed numerous reports, including the annual report of the representative church body
General synod 1871: Master Brooke's committee: draft report. For private circulation among members of sub-committee only
Church of Ireland, general synod 1871, papers by members of Master Brooke's committee
Irish church directory and year book, 1872. Though not strictly an official publication it contains much material drawn from official sources

NEWSPAPERS AND MAGAZINES

Church of Ireland gazette, 1900
Daily Express
Hermathena
*Irish church quarterly,*1908–17
Irish ecclesiastical gazette, 1860–99
Irish Times
Light and Life
The Times

OTHER PRINTED MATERIALS

Akenson, D. H., *The Church of Ireland, ecclesiastical reform and revolution 1800–1885,* New Haven and London, 1971
Alcock, D., *Walking with God: a memoir of the Venerable John Alcock,* London, 1886
Alexander, E., *Primate Alexander, archbishop of Armagh: a memoir,* London, 1913
Ashwell, A. R. and Wilberforce, R. G., *Life of the Rt Rev. Samuel Wilberforce,* 3 vols, London, 1882
Bell, P. M. H., *Disestablishment in Ireland and Wales,* London, 1969
Benson, A. C., *The Life of Edward White Benson, sometime archbishop of Canterbury,* London, 1899
Bernard, J. H., *Archbishop Benson in Ireland,* London, 1896
Bernard, J. H., *The present position of the Irish church,* London, 1904
Birmingham, G. A., *Irishmen all,* London, 1913

Bibliography

Breene, R. S., *The golden jubilee book of Saint Peter's church, Belfast. 1900–1950*, Belfast, 1950

Butcher, S., *A charge delivered to the clergy of the diocese of Meath* ..., Dublin, 1867

Cairnes, T. P., *Statement* ... *made on behalf of the Church of Ireland sustentation fund*, Dublin, 1877

Carroll, W. G., *A memoir of the Rt Rev. James Thomas O'Brien*, Dublin, 1875

Chatterton, E., *The story of fifty years' mission work in Chota Nagpur*, London, 1901

The church and the curates: a statement ..., 2nd ed., Dublin, 1872

Cooke-Trench, T., *An autobiography to which is appended an account of the church of Saint Michael and All Angels at Clane*, Galway, n.d.

Cuming, G. J., *A history of anglican liturgy*, London, 1969

Dann, A. G., *George Webster: a memoir*, Dublin, 1892

D'Arcy, C. F., *The adventures of a bishop*, London, 1934

Davidson, R. T. and Benham, W., *Life of Archibald Campbell Tait*, 2 vols, London, 1891

Dawson, A. H., *A short account of St Bartholomew's church*, Dublin, 1871

Day, J. G. F. and Patton, H. E., *The cathedrals of the Church of Ireland*, Dublin, 1932

Ewald, A. C., *Life and letters of Sir Joseph Napier*, 1st ed., London, 1887, 2nd ed., London, 1892

Ferguson, M. C., *Life of the Right Rev. William Reeves*, Dublin, 1893

Fitzgerald, W., *The duties of the parochial clergy: a charge* ..., London, 1857

Fitzgerald, W., *The revival of synods in the united Church of England and Ireland. A charge* ..., London, 1861

Fox, R. M., *History of the Irish Citizen Army*, Dublin, 1944

French, R. B. D., 'J. O. Hannay and the Gaelic League', *Hermathena*, cii, pp. 26–52

Gathorne-Hardy, A. E., *Gathorne Hardy, first earl of Cranbrook*, 2 vols, London, 1910

Godkin, J., *Ireland amd her churches*, London, 1867

Greer, J., *A questioning generation*, Belfast, 1970

Gregg, J., *A charge* ..., 2nd ed., Dublin, 1867

Gregg, R. S., *Memorials of the life of John Gregg*, Dublin, 1879

Gwynn, S., *Ulster*, Edinburgh, 1911

Hannay, J. O., *The life of Frederick Richards Wynne*, London, 1897

Hannay, J. O., *Pleasant places*, London, 1934

Harford Battersley, C. F., *Pilkington of Uganda*, London, 1899

Henson, H. H., *Retrospect of an unimportant life*, 3 vols, London, 1942–50

Hurley, M., ed., *Irish anglicanism 1869–1969, essays on the role of anglicanism in Irish life presented to the Church of Ireland on the occasion of its disestablishment, by a group of methodist, presbyterian, quaker and Roman catholic scholars*, Dublin, 1970

Independent Television Authority, *Religion in Britain and Northern Ireland: a survey of popular attitudes*, London, 1970

Bibliography

Leslie, J. B., *Armagh clergy and parishes: being an account of the clergy of the Church of Ireland in the diocese of Armagh, from the earliest period, with historical notices of the several parishes, churches, etc.*, Dundalk, 1911

Leslie, J. B., *Ossory clergy and parishes: being an account of the clergy of the Church of Ireland in the diocese of Ossory, from the earliest period, with historical notices of the several parishes, churches, etc.*, Enniskillen, 1933

Leslie, J. B., *Biographical succession lists of the clergy of the diocese of Down*, Enniskillen, 1936

Leslie, J. B., *Derry clergy and parishes, being an account of the clergy of the Church of Ireland in the diocese of Derry, from the earliest period, with historical notices of the several parishes, churches, etc.*, Enniskillen, 1937

Leslie, J. B., *Ardfert and Aghadoe clergy and parishes: being an account of the clergy of the Church of Ireland in the diocese of Ardfert and Aghadoe from the earliest period, with historical notices of the several parishes, churches, etc.*, Dublin, 1940

Leslie, J. B., *Raphoe clergy and parishes, being an account of the clergy of the Church of Ireland in the diocese of Raphoe, from the earliest period, with historical notices of the several parishes, churches, etc.*, Enniskillen, 1940

Lucas, R. J., *Colonel Saunderson, MP: a memoir*, London, 1908

MacColl, M., *Memoirs and correspondence*, ed. G. W. E. Russell, London, 1914

McDermott, R. P. and Webb, D. A., *Irish protestantism today and tomorrow: a demographic study*, Dublin, 1945

MacDonnell, J. C., *Life and correspondence of W. C. Magee*, 2 vols, London, 1896

MacNeice, J. F., *The Church of Ireland in Belfast*, Belfast, 1931

MacNeill, M. C. D., *A blessed life: being a biographical sketch of the Rev. J. G. S. MacNeill*, Dublin, 1891

Madden, I., *Memoir of the Rt Rev. Robert Daly*, London, 1875

Maguire, E., *Fifty years of clerical life in the Church of Ireland*, Dublin, 1904

Mahaffy, J. P., 'About Irish church music', *Irish church quarterly*, i, p. 93

Milne, K., *St Bartholomew's: a history of a Dublin parish*, Dublin, 1963

Milner, W. S., *The revision of canon thirty-six*, Carrickfergus, 1967

Monypenny, W. F. and Buckle, G. E., *The life of Benjamin Disraeli, earl of Beaconsfield*, 6 vols, London, 1910–20

Murray, R. H., *Archbishop Bernard: professor, prelate, provost*, London, 1931

Norman, E. R., *The catholic church and Ireland in the age of rebellion*, London, 1965

O'Brien, J. T., *The case of the established church in Ireland*, Dublin, 1867

O'Brien, R. B., *The life of Charles Stewart Parnell*, 2 vols, London, 1898

Osborne, C. E., *Life of Father Dolling*, London, 1903

Patton, H. E., *Fifty years of disestablishment: a sketch of the history of the Church of Ireland, 1869–1920*, Dublin, 1922

Phillips, W. A., *History of the Church of Ireland from the earliest times to the present day*, 3 vols, Oxford, 1933–4

Robinson, L., *Palette and plough*, Dublin, 1948

Robinson, R., ed., *Speeches delivered in the general convention of the Church of Ireland by the Rev. Romney Robinson and the bishop of Ossory*, Dublin, 1870

Reports and papers relating to the life table on which the life of the clergy of the Church of Ireland should be calculated, ordered to be printed by the representative body of the Church of Ireland, Dublin, 1871

Seaver, G., *John Allen Fitzgerald Gregg, archbishop*, London, 1963

Sherlock, W., *Church organization*, Dublin, 1868

Sherlock, W., 'The story of the revision of the Irish prayer book', in *Irish church quarterly*, iii, pp. 12–32, 144–66

Stanford, W. B., *A recognized church: the Church of Ireland in Eire*, Dublin, 1944

Stopford, E. A., *Lord Dufferin and the church in Ireland*, Dublin, 1867

Stopford, E. A., *To the clergy and laity: subjects for thought concerning the future of the Church of Ireland* . . ., Dublin, 1868

Street, G. E., *The cathedral of the Holy Trinity called Christ Church* . . . *an account of the restoration of the fabric*, London, 1882

Sumner, G. H., ed., *Principles at stake: essays on church questions of the day*, 2nd ed., London, 1868

Thompson, H. M. and Bigger, F. J., *The cathedral church of Belfast*, Belfast, 1923

Traill, A., 'Irish church finance since disestablishment', in *Irish church quarterly*, i, pp. 3–8, 112–22

Trench, M., *Richard Chenevix Trench, archbishop: letters and memorials*, 2 vols, London, 1888

Trench, R. C., *A charge* . . ., Dublin, 1871

Trench, R. C., *A charge* . . ., Dublin, 1875

Trevelyan, G. M., *Life of John Bright*, London, 1913

Trollope, A., *Clergymen of the Church of England*, London, 1866

Walsh, B. M., *Religion and demographic behaviour in Ireland*, Dublin, 1970

Webster, G., *An address to the parishioners of Saint Nicholas*, Cork, 1863

Webster, G., *Amusements: a lecture*, Dublin, 1859

White, H. V., *List of SPG missionaries, 1701–1895, of Irish parentage*, 1895

White, N. J. D., *John Henry Bernard* . . . *a short memoir*, Dublin, 1928

Wynne, F. R., *Spent in the service: a memoir of the Very Rev. Achilles Daunt*, London, 1879

INDEX

~~~~~~~~~~~~~~~~~~~~~~~~~~~~~~~~~

153

Index

Canterbury, Archbishop of, *see*
Benson, Edward White; Longley,
Charles Thomas; Tait,
Archibald Campbell
Carnarvon, *see* Herbert, Henry
Howard Molyneux
Carroll, William George, 10, 59
Carson, Joseph, 82–3
Carysfort, *see* Proby, William
Cashel, bishop of, *see* Daly, Robert;
O'Hara, Henry Stewart
Cashel, synod of, 1
Cassels, Andrew, 96
Cathedrals, 12–13, 78, 80
Chadwick, John Alexander, 73
Charles, Robert Henry, 89
Chichester, Edward, Lord
(subsequently 4th Marquess of
Donegall), 14
Chota Nagpur Mission, 93
Church-building, 79
Church education society, 22–3
Church of Ireland: constitution of,
54–7, 98, 103; finances of,
66–70, 128–9; parochial
structure of, 11, 73, 129–30;
and Christian unity, 90–1; and
divorce, 112–13; and education,
21–3, 114–18; and Home Rule,
98–100; and Irish language
movement, 102–3, 115–16;
and Methodist church, 135;
and missionary work, 92–4;
and presbyterian church, 90–2,
134–5; and recruiting, 106–7;
and reunion, 89–90, 135;
and ritualism, 58–60, 87–9,
134; and social questions, 90–2;
and Spanish and Portuguese
churches, 94–7; and Ulster
unionists, 104
Clergy: education of, 13–17, 84–5,
130; incomes and distribution
of, 11–12, 74, 124–6, 129
Clogher, bishop of, *see* Loftus,
Robert Ponsonby Tottenham;
Stack, Charles Maurice
Collins, James Stratford, 93

Collins, Michael, 110
Collins, William Henry, 93
Connor, bishop of, *see* Irwin,
Charles King
Convocation, 1–2; of Canterbury,
42; Irish, 30, 37
Cooke-Trench, Thomas Richard
Frederick, 79
Cork, 20–1, 80
Cork, bishop of, *see* Gregg, John;
Meade, William Edward
Cosgrave, William Thomas, 110
Crozier, John Baptist, 89, 91, 105

Daly, Robert, 10
D'Arcy, Charles Frederick, 73,
104, 134
D'Arcy, Thomas Lavallin, 59
Daunt, Achilles, 17–18
De Montmorency, Hervey, 4th
Viscount Mountmorres, 13
Denny, Edward, 61
Derby, *see* Stanley, Edward
George Geoffrey Smith
Derry, bishop of, *see* Alexander,
William; Chadwick, George
Alexander
Dickinson, Hercules Henry, 21, 60
Dillyn, Lewis Llewellyn, 27–8
Disraeli, Benjamin, 28, 32–3,
35–6, 44
Dolling, Robert William
Radclyffe, 88, 89
Dowden, John, 89
Down, bishop of, *see* D'Arcy,
Charles Frederick; Kerr,
William Shaw; Knox, Robert
Bent; Welland, Thomas James
Dowse, Richard, 94
Drew, Thomas, 19
Drew, Thomas, 77
Dublin, 19, 75–6, 105, 107–8
Dublin, Archbishop of, *see* Barton,
Arthur William; Bernard, John
Henry; Peacocke, Joseph
Ferguson; Plunket, William
Conyngham; Trench, Richard
Chenevix; Whately, Richard